Writers in Residence

Answer Key and Teaching Notes

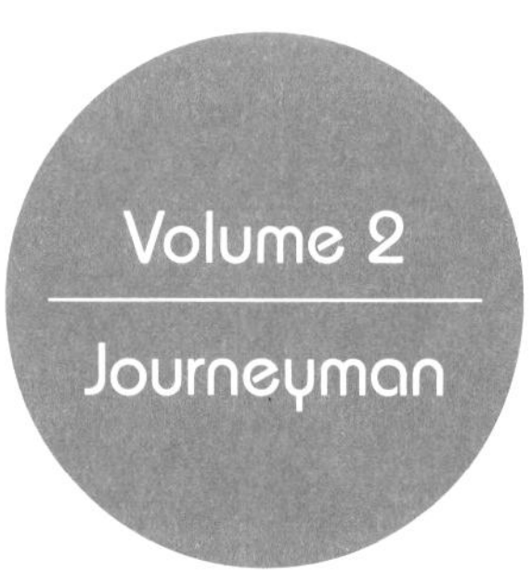

by Debra Bell, PhD

with Joanna Breault

Apologia Educational Ministries, Inc.

WRITERS IN RESIDENCE ANSWER KEY, VOLUME 2

Published by
Apologia Educational Ministries
1106 Meridian Plaza, Suite 220/340
Anderson, Indiana 46016
www.apologia.com

Manufactured in the USA
First Printing: August 2017

ISBN: 978-1-940110-33-2

Cover Design: Doug Powell
Book Design: Holly Grundon

Printed by LSC Communications

Contents

Note: No answer key is required for module 2.

How to use the Answer Key and Teaching Notes

Writers in Residence
TAKES THE PAIN OUT OF
Teaching Kids to Write!

This book is your road map to using *Writers in Residence*, volume 2. You will find all the tools you need to do the following:

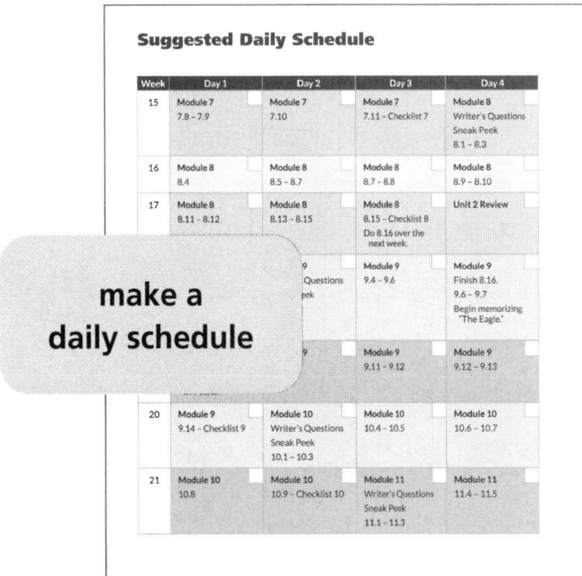

Suggested Daily Schedule

Week	Day 1	Day 2	Day 3	Day 4
15	Module 7 7.8 – 7.9	Module 7 7.10	Module 7 7.11 – Checklist 7	Module 8 Writer's Questions Sneak Peek 8.1 – 8.3
16	Module 8 8.4	Module 8 8.5 – 8.7	Module 8 8.7 – 8.8	Module 8 8.9 – 8.10
17	Module 8 8.11 – 8.12	Module 8 8.13 – 8.15	Module 8 8.15 – Checklist 8 Do 8.16 over the next week.	Unit 2 Review
		9 Questions ek	Module 9 9.4 – 9.6	Module 9 Finish 8.16. 9.6 – 9.7 Begin memorizing "The Eagle."
		9	Module 9 9.11 – 9.12	Module 9 9.12 – 9.13
20	Module 9 9.14 – Checklist 9	Module 10 Writer's Questions Sneak Peek 10.1 – 10.3	Module 10 10.4 – 10.5	Module 10 10.6 – 10.7
21	Module 10 10.8	Module 10 10.9 – Checklist 10	Module 11 Writer's Questions Sneak Peek 11.1 – 11.3	Module 11 11.4 – 11.5

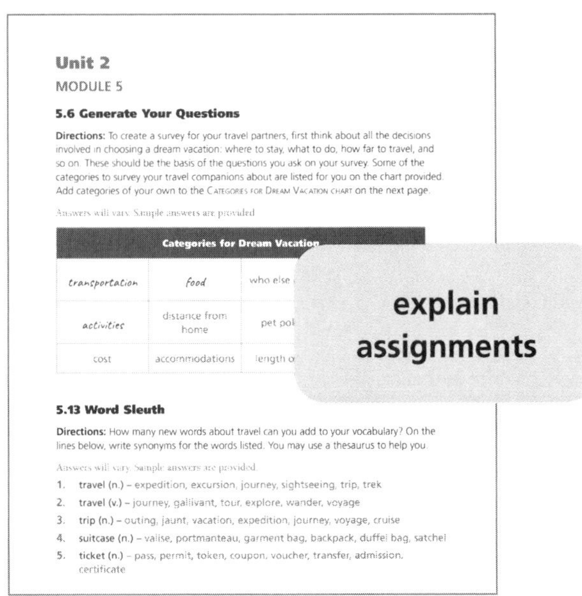

Unit 2

MODULE 5

5.6 Generate Your Questions

Directions: To create a survey for your travel partners, first think about all the decisions involved in choosing a dream vacation: where to stay, what to do, how far to travel, and so on. These should be the basis of the questions you ask on your survey. Some of the categories to survey your travel companions about are listed for you on the chart provided. Add categories of your own to the Categories for Dream Vacation chart on the next page.

Answers will vary. Sample answers are provided.

Categories for Dream Vacation		
transportation	food	who else
activities	distance from home	pet pol
cost	accommodations	length o

5.13 Word Sleuth

Directions: How many new words about travel can you add to your vocabulary? On the lines below, write synonyms for the words listed. You may use a thesaurus to help you.

Answers will vary. Sample answers are provided.

1. travel (n.) – expedition, excursion, journey, sightseeing, trip, trek
2. travel (v.) – journey, gallivant, tour, explore, wander, voyage
3. trip (n.) – outing, jaunt, vacation, expedition, journey, voyage, cruise
4. suitcase (n.) – valise, portmanteau, garment bag, backpack, duffel bag, satchel
5. ticket (n.) – pass, permit, token, coupon, voucher, transfer, admission, certificate

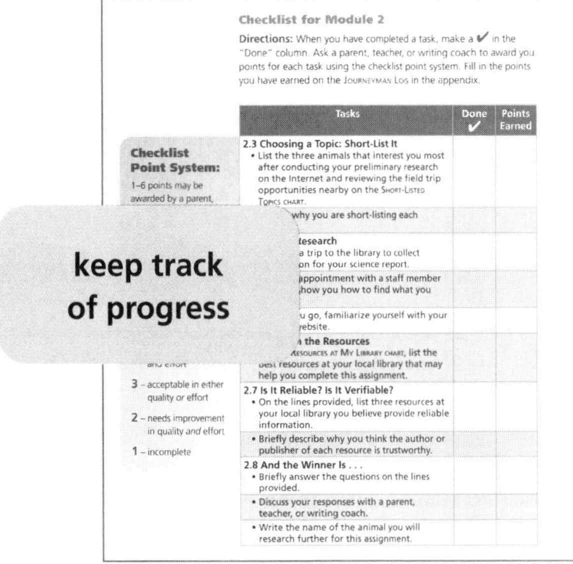

Checklist for Module 2

Directions: When you have completed a task, make a ✔ in the "Done" column. Ask a parent, teacher, or writing coach to award you points for each task using the checklist point system. Fill in the points you have earned on the Journeyman Log in the appendix.

Checklist Point System:

1–6 points may be awarded by a parent,

and effort

3 – acceptable in either quality *or* effort

2 – needs improvement in quality *and* effort

1 – incomplete

Tasks	Done ✔	Points Earned
2.3 Choosing a Topic: Short-List It • List the three animals that interest you most after conducting your preliminary research on the Internet and reviewing the field trip opportunities nearby on the Short-Listed Topics chart.		
why you are short-listing each		
esearch a trip to the library to collect on for your science report.		
appointment with a staff member how you how to find what you		
u go, familiarize yourself with your website.		
the Resources Resources at My Library chart, list the best resources at your local library that may help you complete this assignment.		
2.7 Is It Reliable? Is It Verifiable? • On the lines provided, list three resources at your local library you believe provide reliable information.		
• Briefly describe why you think the author or publisher of each resource is trustworthy.		
2.8 And the Winner Is . . . • Briefly answer the questions on the lines provided.		
• Discuss your responses with a parent, teacher, or writing coach.		
• Write the name of the animal you will research further for this assignment.		

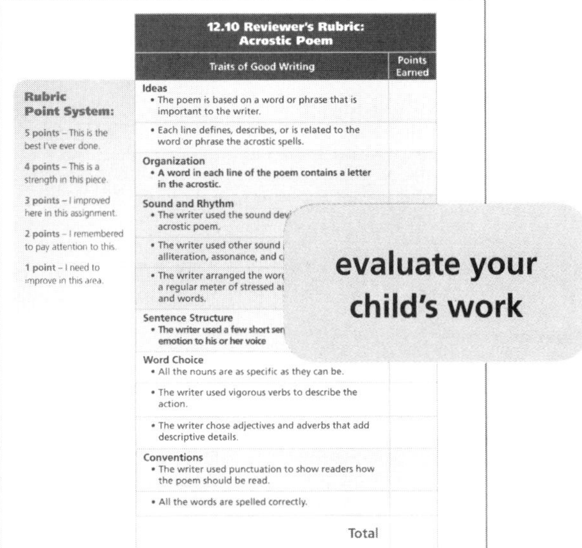

Rubric Point System:

5 points – This is the best I've ever done.

4 points – This is a strength in this piece.

3 points – I improved here in this assignment.

2 points – I remembered to pay attention to this.

1 point – I need to improve in this area.

12.10 Reviewer's Rubric: Acrostic Poem	
Traits of Good Writing	**Points Earned**
Ideas • The poem is based on a word or phrase that is important to the writer.	
• Each line defines, describes, or is related to the word or phrase the acrostic spells.	
Organization • A word in each line of the poem contains a letter in the acrostic.	
Sound and Rhythm • The writer used the sound dev acrostic poem.	
• The writer used other sound alliteration, assonance, and c	
• The writer arranged the wor a regular meter of stressed a and words.	
Sentence Structure • The writer used a few short sen emotion to his or her voice	
Word Choice • All the nouns are as specific as they can be.	
• The writer used vigorous verbs to describe the action.	
• The writer chose adjectives and adverbs that add descriptive details.	
Conventions • The writer used punctuation to show readers how the poem should be read.	
• All the words are spelled correctly.	
Total	

Teaching Notes

This section lists all activities in each unit where students are instructed to ask a parent, teacher, or writing coach to assist them. I also explain the overall goal of each writing assignment, highlight activities that require you to plan ahead, and provide background information about the major topics in each unit.

Answers

This book contains answers or sample answers for the following student activities from the Student Text and Workbook:

activities where one correct answer is required

activities where answers may vary, but a set range of answers is acceptable

activities where a student is asked to give examples

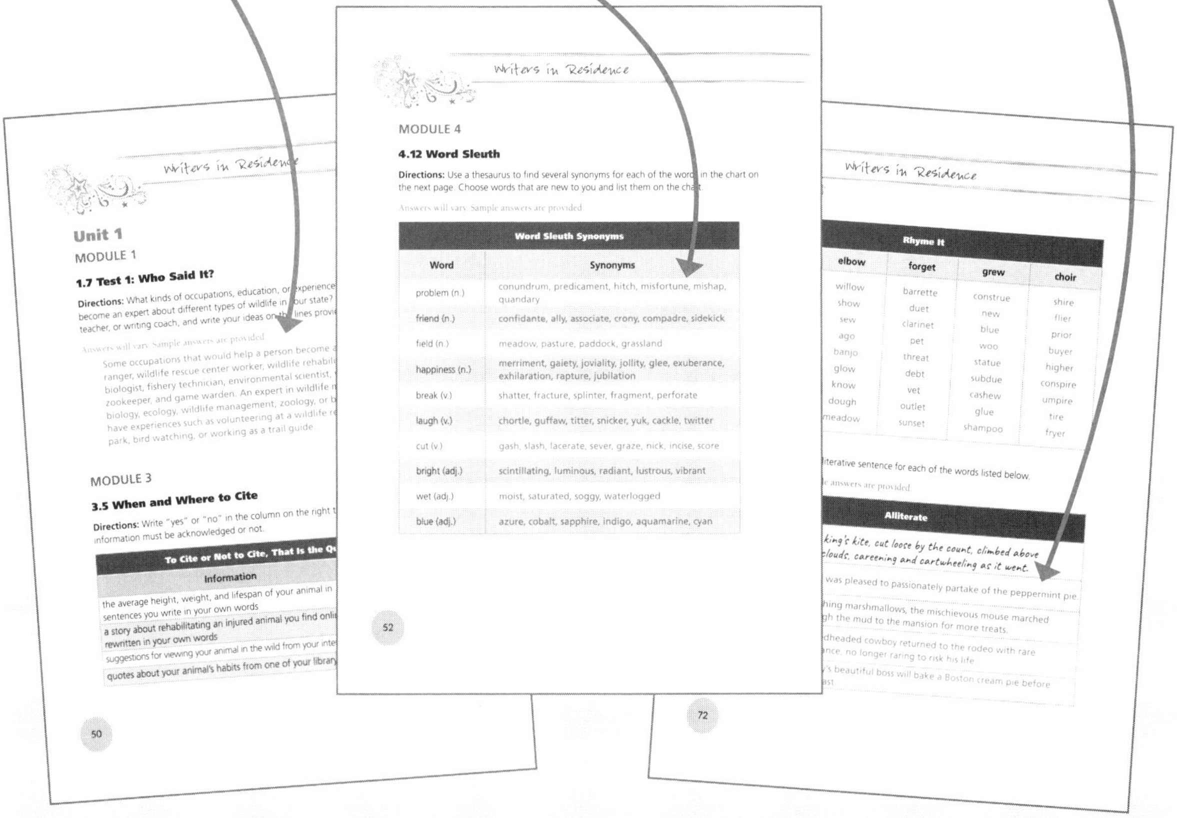

Writers in Residence

MODULE 4

4.12 Word Sleuth

Directions: Use a thesaurus to find several synonyms for each of the words in the chart on the next page. Choose words that are new to you and list them on the chart.

Answers will vary. Sample answers are provided.

Word Sleuth Synonyms	
Word	**Synonyms**
problem (n.)	conundrum, predicament, hitch, misfortune, mishap, quandary
friend (n.)	confidante, ally, associate, crony, compadre, sidekick
field (n.)	meadow, pasture, paddock, grassland
happiness (n.)	merriment, gaiety, joviality, jollity, glee, exuberance, exhilaration, rapture, jubilation
break (v.)	shatter, fracture, splinter, fragment, perforate
laugh (v.)	chortle, guffaw, titter, snicker, yuk, cackle, twitter
cut (v.)	gash, slash, lacerate, sever, graze, nick, incise, score
bright (adj.)	scintillating, luminous, radiant, lustrous, vibrant
wet (adj.)	moist, saturated, soggy, waterlogged
blue (adj.)	azure, cobalt, sapphire, indigo, aquamarine, cyan

52

Writers in Residence
TAKES THE MYSTERY OUT OF EVALUATING
What Your Kids Write!

Rubrics

Use the Student's Rubric at the beginning of each unit in the Student Text and Workbook to direct your child's attention to the requirements of each writing assignment.

A rubric is a special checklist for evaluating and grading writing or other projects.

Rubrics for both the student and reviewers are specifically designed to match each unit's writing assignment.

The Student's Rubric for each unit appears in the introduction and again in the last module of the unit in the Student Text and Workbook. The Student's Rubrics are reproduced for your reference on pages 118–228 of this book.

The rubric is organized using the six traits of good writing. See pages xxii–xxxiii of the Student Text and Workbook and page 20 of this book for more information about the six traits writing model.

Bulleted points tell students the specific characteristics of each trait to include in the assignment.

Rubric Point System:

5 points – This is the best I've ever done.

4 points – This is a strength in this piece.

3 points – I improved here in this assignment.

2 points – I remembered to pay attention to this.

1 point – I need to improve in this area.

Student's Rubric for "Into the Wild"

Traits of Good Writing	Points Earned
Word Choice • All my nouns are as specific as they can be.*	
• I used vigorous verbs to describe the action.*	
• I chose adjectives and adverbs that add descriptive details.*	
• I used interrogative adverbs and interrogative pronouns to create questions about my animal.	
Conventions • I properly documented my sources in the body of my report.	
• I properly documented my sources in the bibliography.	
• I properly alphabetized my list of sources in the bibliography.	
• I followed the rules for capitalization carefully, especially in my titles.	
• I punctuated my direct quotations correctly.	
• I punctuated the end of each sentence correctly, including my questions.*	
• I checked to make sure all my words are spelled correctly.	
Total	

Unit 1: 120 points possible

Student's Rubric for "A Fantastical Tale of Extraordinary Exploits"	
Traits of Good Writing	**Points Earned**
Ideas • I created a fantastical setting.	4
• I included details and dialogue that reveal the setting to my readers at the beginning of the story.	3
• I developed a plot with a main problem that is not too big or too small to be introduced and resolved in my story.	4
• I created a main character that my readers care about.	3
• I created a cast of characters that includes talking animals or imaginary creatures.	3
Organization • I created an opening hook that engages my readers' interest and attention.	4
• I included an inciting incident that introduces the main problem.	5
• Each sentence fulfills a clear purpose in the paragraph.	3
• My plot includes exposition, rising action, climax, falling action, and resolution.	3
Voice • I created a narrator with a distinct voice.	3
• I used a consistent point of view throughout the story.	4
• I gave my major characters distinct voices that reveal their character traits.	3
• I chose words for their connotations and used punctuation to add meaning, emotion, and cadence to my narrator's and other characters' voices.	4
Sentence Structure • I used transitions to connect my ideas or signal my readers about what is coming next.*	5
• I varied the length of my sentences to show when my characters are speaking slowly and when they are speaking more quickly.	4
Word Choice • All my nouns are as specific as they can be.*	3
• I used vigorous verbs to describe the action.*	4
• I chose adjectives and adverbs that add descriptive details.*	4
• The antecedents of pronouns are clear and nearby.	3
Conventions • I followed the rules for capitalization carefully.*	5
• I properly punctuated the dialogue between characters.*	3
• My pronouns are in agreement with other parts of the sentence.	4
• I checked to make sure all my words are spelled correctly.	5
Total	86

Unit 4: 115 points possible

Rubric Point System:

5 points – This is the best I've ever done.

4 points – This is a strength in this piece.

3 points – I improved here in this assignment.

2 points – I remembered to pay attention to this.

1 point – I need to improve in this area.

Scoring

The five-point rubric scoring system emphasizes "progress, not perfection" as the goal.

Student's Rubrics help students learn how to evaluate their own writing and track their progress. Students discuss the strengths and weaknesses of each piece with a parent, teacher, or writing coach before deciding how many points they should receive.

The rubrics for later units expand as new traits are introduced and previously taught traits and skills are reinforced and practiced.

A reviewer's version of each rubric is provided in the appendix of the Student Text and Workbook and in the back of this book. Parents, teachers, and other readers can use **Reviewer's Rubrics** to to give the student feedback on each completed writing assignment. (Only the points earned on the Student's Rubric, however, are filled in on the Journeyman Log.)

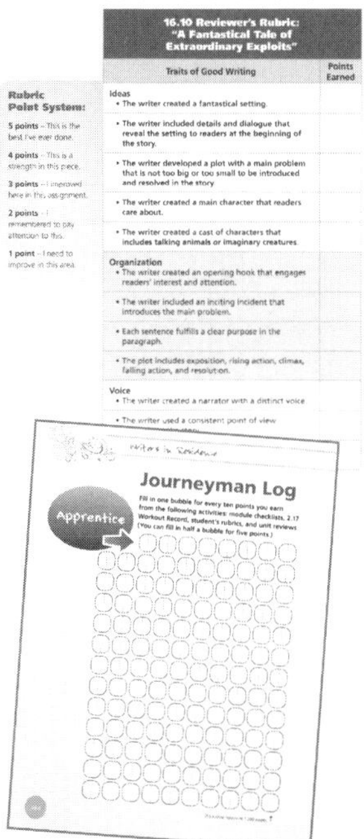

Students may fill in their total points on the **Journeyman Log** in the appendix of the Student Text and Workbook.

Checklists

Use the checklist at the end of each module in the Student Text and Workbook to direct your child's attention to every task that must be completed in the module.

Checklist for Module 13

Directions: When you have completed a task, make a ✔ in the "Done" column. Ask a parent, teacher, or writing coach to award you points for each task using the checklist point system. Fill in the points you have earned on the Journeyman Log in the appendix.

Checklist Point System:

1–6 points may be awarded by a parent, teacher, or writing coach for each task completed. Here are the recommended guidelines:

6 – exemplary in quality *and* effort

5 – exemplary in either quality *or* effort

4 – acceptable in quality *and* effort

3 – acceptable in either quality *or* effort

2 – needs improvement in quality *and* effort

1 – incomplete

Tasks	Done ✔	Points Earned
13.2 Why Imagine? • Talk with a parent, teacher, or writing coach about why you think God gave you an imagination. Take time to thank Him for your fantastic imagination and ask Him to help you use it in new and surprising ways in this unit.		
13.3 The Writing Process • Use the infographic "Introduction to the Writing Process" to answer the questions.		
13.4 Know Your Readers • Name the young listener for whom your story will be written. Include his or her age.		
• Describe some of the things you know about this person. Include some of the books, movies, and activities you know this person likes. If you have a picture of your young listener, then affix it in the space provided.		
13.5 Far and Away • Study the opening pages of a book with a fantastical setting and answer the questions.		
13.6 The Setting Is in the Details • Fill out the Setting chart with some of the ideas you have about your fantastical time and place.		
• After you have decided on some of the details, choose a memorable name for this fantasyland and include it on the Setting chart. Also write the name of the child for whom you are creating this tale.		

Student Copies

The checklist at the end of each module in the Student Text and Workbook helps students to stay on track and to complete all assignments.

Parent Copies

The checklists are reproduced on pages 140–175 of this book. Use these checklists to track progress and evaluate student work.

Scoring System

After students complete each assignment in the module, a parent, teacher, or writing coach should use the six-point scoring system to award points based on their effort and quality of work. Students may fill in the points they are awarded on the Journeyman Log in the appendix of the Student Text and Workbook.

Student Tasks

The checklist includes every task the student must complete in the module.

Guidelines for Evaluation

A guiding principle of the *Writers in Residence* series is "progress, not perfection." With this in mind, begin any evaluation of your child's work by considering his or her age and experience. Your feedback and the points you may award should always be based on a comparison of *this* work with your child's prior work. Use the point systems for both the rubrics and checklists to set a standard for the student to reach toward.

Targeted Feedback + Praise = Progress

For maximum benefit, any evaluation of the student's work should be accompanied by targeted feedback. Targeted feedback is specific and concrete. For example, you might say, "The verb *rambled* in this sentence is very strong. I can picture the action precisely. Can you think of a verb to replace *said* in the next sentence that is just as precise?"

Praise—such as "This is excellent!" or "You've worked very hard, and I am so pleased"—is important, but this is not feedback. Praise is a source of encouragement—a gift we should give generously to our children. However, praise in the absence of targeted feedback doesn't help kids improve; it only helps them to keep putting forth effort. You will notice that the checklist point system is based on *quality* and *effort*. Parents, teachers, and writing coaches help students reach both of these goals with the powerful combination of praise and targeted feedback—and that produces progress.

Talk about It, Talk about It, Talk about It

So how should you proceed when a student's answer is wrong or wide of the mark? Simply talk about it—a lot. Ask questions, draw the student out, and try to get to the bottom of his or her erroneous thinking or lack of appropriate effort. Use the assignments in WIR as discussion starters. If students know you will devote time to talk with them as you evaluate the quality and effort of their work, they will put more time into the task in the first place. Where parents, teachers, and writing coaches commit their time shows students what is most important. So distribute your time wisely.

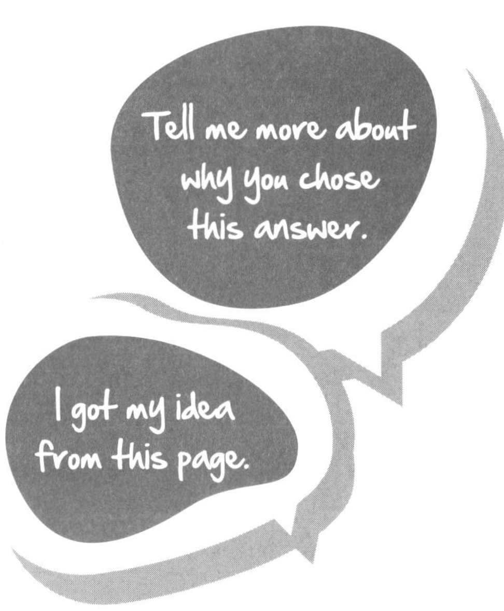

Tell me more about why you chose this answer.
I got my idea from this page.

Suggested Daily Schedule

Note: Some assignments are allotted more than one day for completion. Also, many students may wish to invest more time in writing assignments that especially interest them. Please allow students to spend as much time on an assignment as they like. Writing a lot is more important than sticking to the suggested schedule. Activities that require planning ahead are highlighted in blue.

Week	Day 1	Day 2	Day 3	Day 4
1	**Introduction** Welcome to *Writers in Residence*! Spotlight on Christian Writers	**Infographics** Study and discuss the infographics (pages xxii–xxv).	**Intro to Unit 1** Read and discuss "Meet Sherri Seligson." Read "Introduction: Into the Wild." Note "Plan Ahead." Study the rubric.	**Module 1** Writer's Questions Sneak Peek 1.1 – 1.4
2	**Module 1** 1.5 – 1.8	**Module 1** 1.9 – 1.11	**Module 1** 1.12 – 1.13	**Module 1** 1.14 – 1.15
3	**Module 1** 1.15 – Checklist 1	**Module 2** Writer's Questions Sneak Peek 2.1 – 2.4	**Module 2** 2.5 – 2.7 Library Visit	**Module 2** 2.8 – 2.9
4	**Module 2** 2.10 – 2.11	**Module 2** 2.12 – 2.14	**Module 2** 2.15 – 2.17, 2.20	**Module 2** Study
5	**Module 2** Study	**Module 2** Study	**Module 2** 2.18 – 2.19	**Module 2** 2.19 Field Trip
6	**Module 2** Finish 2.20 – Checklist 2	**Module 3** Writer's Questions Sneak Peek 3.1 – 3.4	**Module 3** 3.5 – 3.6	**Module 3** 3.7 – 3.8
7	**Module 3** 3.9	**Module 3** 3.10	**Module3** 3.11	**Module 3** 3.12 – Checklist 3

Suggested Daily Schedule

Week	Day 1	Day 2	Day 3	Day 4
8	**Module 4** Writer's Questions Sneak Peek 4.1 – 4.3	**Module 4** 4.4 – 4.5	**Module 4** 4.5 – 4.7	**Module 4** 4.8
9	**Module 4** 4.9 – 4.10	**Module 4** 4.10	**Module 4** Do 4.11 over the next week. 4.12 – Checklist 4	**Unit 1 Review**
10	**Intro to Unit 2** Read and discuss "Meet Jenny L. Cote." Read "Introduction: Making the Case." Study the rubric.	**Module 5** Writer's Questions Sneak Peek 5.1 – 5.4	**Module 5** 5.5 – 5.6	**Module 5** Finish 4.11. 5.7
11	**Module 5** 5.8 – 5.9	**Module 5** 5.10 Interviews	**Module 5** 5.11	**Module 5** 5.12 – Checklist 5
12	**Module 6** Writer's Questions Sneak Peek 6.1 – 6.4	**Module 6** 6.5	**Module 6** 6.6 – 6.7	**Module 6** 6.8 – 6.9
13	**Module 6** 6.10	**Module 6** 6.10	**Module 6** 6.11	**Module 6** 6.12
14	**Module 6** 6.13 – Checklist 6	**Module 7** Writer's Questions Sneak Peek 7.1 – 7.3	**Module 7** 7.4 – 7.5	**Module 7** 7.6 – 7.7

Suggested Daily Schedule

Week	Day 1	Day 2	Day 3	Day 4
15	**Module 7** 7.8 – 7.9	**Module 7** 7.10	**Module 7** 7.11 – Checklist 7	**Module 8** Writer's Questions Sneak Peek 8.1 – 8.3
16	**Module 8** 8.4	**Module 8** 8.5 – 8.7	**Module 8** 8.7 – 8.8	**Module 8** 8.9 – 8.10
17	**Module 8** 8.11 – 8.12	**Module 8** 8.13 – 8.15	**Module 8** 8.15 – Checklist 8 Do 8.16 over the next week.	**Unit 2 Review**
18	**Intro to Unit 3** Read and discuss "Meet Phil Lollar." Read "Introduction: Poetry Jam." Study the rubrics.	**Module 9** Writer's Questions Sneak Peek 9.1 – 9.3	**Module 9** 9.4 – 9.6	**Module 9** Finish 8.16. 9.6 – 9.7 Begin memorizing "The Eagle."
19	**Module 9** 9.8 – 9.9 Recite "The Eagle" this week.	**Module 9** 9.10	**Module 9** 9.11 – 9.12	**Module 9** 9.12 – 9.13
20	**Module 9** 9.14 – Checklist 9	**Module 10** Writer's Questions Sneak Peek 10.1 – 10.3	**Module 10** 10.4 – 10.5	**Module 10** 10.6 – 10.7
21	**Module 10** 10.8	**Module 10** 10.9 – Checklist 10	**Module 11** Writer's Questions Sneak Peek 11.1 – 11.3	**Module 11** 11.4 – 11.5

Suggested Daily Schedule

Week	Day 1	Day 2	Day 3	Day 4
22	**Module 11** 11.6 – 11.7	**Module 11** 11.8 – 11.9	**Module 11** 11.10	**Module 11** 11.11 – Checklist 11
23	**Module 12** Writer's Questions Sneak Peek 12.1 – 12.3 Schedule your poetry jam.	**Module 12** 12.4 – 12.5	Module 12 12.5 – 12.7	**Module 12** 12.8 – 12.10
24	**Module 12** 12.11	**Module 12** 12.12	**Module 12** 12.14 – Checklist 12 Do 12.13 over the next week.	**Unit 3 Review**
25	**Intro to Unit 4** Read and discuss "Meet Andrew Peterson." Read "Introduction: A Fantastical Tale of Extraordinary Exploits." Note "Plan Ahead." Study the rubric.	**Module 13** Writer's Questions Sneak Peek 13.1 – 13.3	**Module 13** 13.4 – 13.5	**Module 13** Finish 12.13. 13.6 – 13.7
26	**Module 13** 13.7 – 13.8	**Module 13** 13.9	**Module 13** 13.10 – Checklist 13	**Module 14** Writer's Questions Sneak Peek 14.1 – 14.4
27	**Module 14** 14.4 – 14.5	**Module 14** 14.6 – 14.7	**Module 14** 14.8	**Module 14** 14.8

Suggested Daily Schedule

Week	Day 1	Day 2	Day 3	Day 4
28	**Module 14** 14.8	**Module 14** 14.8 – Checklist 14	**Module 15** Writer's Questions Sneak Peek 15.1 – 15.2	**Module 15** 15.3 – 15.4
29	**Module 15** 15.5 – 15.6	**Module 15** 15.7	**Module 15** 15.8	**Module 15** 15.9 – Checklist 15
30	**Module 16** Writer's Questions Sneak Peek 16.1 – 16.3	**Module 16** 16.4	**Module 16** 16.5	**Module 16** 16.6
31	**Module 16** 16.7 – 16.8	**Module 16** 16.8 – 16.9	**Module 16** 16.10 – 16.11 Do 16.12 over the next week.	**Module 16** 16.13 – Checklist 16
32	**Unit 4 Review**	**Final Review**	**Final Review**	**Final Review**

Welcome, parents, teachers, and writing coaches! This introduction includes an overview of the teaching philosophy and methods used throughout the series.

Why *Writers in Residence* Is Unique

Many writing programs ask students to produce four traditional forms of writing: personal, expository, persuasive, and narrative. But authentic writing tasks (the kinds we engage in as adults) rarely fall exclusively into any one of these categories. Rather, most adult writing requires us to combine several forms of writing to achieve our intended purpose and to connect with our readers. The assignments in the *Writers in Residence* series reflect this reality. Over the course of the program, students will learn about and practice the types of writing that adults regularly use for work and for pleasure. At the same time, they will master the concepts and skills necessary to be ready for college by the end of high school.

Each unit features one or more expert models from professional writers, including some well-known authors. Students study specific aspects of the author's craft and then use the model as an inspiration for their own writing assignments.

These are the four types of writing tasks in the *Writers in Residence* series:

I Remember

These writing prompts ask students to write about experiences they have had. They correlate roughly with the traditional personal narrative. Memories and experiences are a rich source of ideas for expert writers. Here is the wellspring of our life stories—unique tales that God is authoring for His purposes and His glory. Not only will students learn to tell the tales that set their lives apart from all others, but they will also learn to think reflectively about the meaning and purpose of these events—and perhaps through the process figure out what God is calling them to next.

I Imagine

These writing prompts are high-interest creative writing assignments. Here students begin to study expert models of fiction closely and learn to include the elements of fiction in their own stories. At the same time, they see that authors often draw on their own memories and experiences as a springboard for many of the stories they weave. Students also learn that a narrative arc is an important strategy writers use to keep readers reading even in a research or argument paper.

I Investigate

These writing prompts introduce research skills and research writing, but with a twist: The research projects in WIR mirror the world of journalism, where field research and interviews are essential sources of information. Students also learn how to detect bias in their sources and their own writing. Finally, young writers learn how to include (not suppress) their own voices in what they report.

I Think

These writing prompts teach students the fundamental elements of argument writing, of which persuasive writing is only a subset. In an argument essay, an author takes a position and defends it with logical reasoning, facts, apt examples, and details. This is the mode of discourse in an academic setting and the most important type of writing students must master if they want to have their ideas considered in a college classroom or the broader culture. Further, learning to write cogent arguments is the best way to help students think more deeply and critically about the ideas, philosophies, and claims circling around them.

How to Make WIR Work for Your Students

WIR is designed to be flexible. Please take advantage of this and set reasonable expectations for each student who uses the *Writers in Residence* series. WIR is challenging but not developmentally inappropriate. Challenge is good. Kids need to break a cognitive sweat if learning is to take place. They need a sense of accomplishment if we want them to take pride in their achievements. However, overchallenging children can be detrimental. They must feel successful, not frustrated. Because of age and developmental readiness, some students will complete a volume in a year; other students may need a year and a half. It is important that students enjoy the writing process and find pleasure in their creative endeavors. Use this priority as a guide to help you set the standard for each child. "Progress, not perfection" should always be the goal.

> "Progress, not perfection" should always be the goal.

You can use the *Writers in Residence* series in several different ways to fit your family's overall needs and each child's readiness and interests:

1. The target age group for volume 1 is fourth grade and up. The target age group for volume 2 is fifth grade and up, and so forth. You can use WIR with several different children at multiple grade levels at the same time. Be sure to adjust your expectations of each child accordingly. You can start the program with a student who is reading chapter books independently.

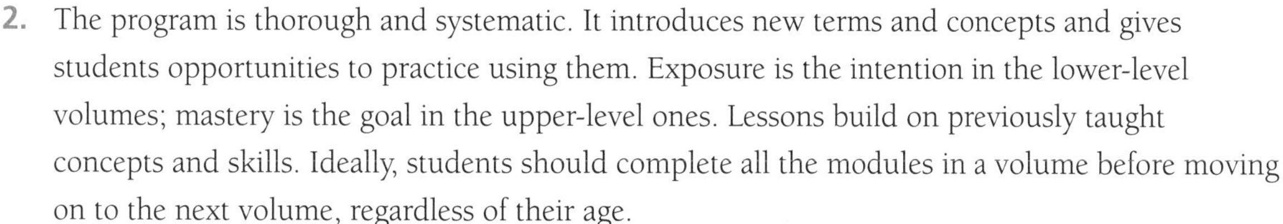

2. The program is thorough and systematic. It introduces new terms and concepts and gives students opportunities to practice using them. Exposure is the intention in the lower-level volumes; mastery is the goal in the upper-level ones. Lessons build on previously taught concepts and skills. Ideally, students should complete all the modules in a volume before moving on to the next volume, regardless of their age.

3. How students complete that work is your choice. WIR includes a lot of questions. For a younger child, writing out answers to all the questions may become a tedious chore. You don't have to require this. It's fine to just talk about some or all of the questions together. In many cases, discussing the writing process and decisions with a student is the best way to help him or her grow as a writer.

4. Students should attempt all the writing assignments since later volumes build on previously taught material. However, if an assignment is too easy, it is fine to ask a student just to read through the material or modify the assignment to create greater challenge or interest. If an assignment is too challenging, it is fine to modify it.

5. The suggested schedule on pages 10–14 shows 128 days of work. This means that students can complete this volume in thirty-two weeks if they work on assignments four days a week. However, this is just one possibility. Students should spend at least three days per week on this program. Younger students may find that spreading the work over five days per week for thirty-six or more weeks is the best plan for staying motivated and managing the challenge.

Co-ops, Writing Groups, and Writing Coaches

The *Writers in Residence* series works well with writing groups. The suggested daily schedule lists assignments for four days per week. The fifth day of any week can then be used for a co-op day or a writing group. In both of these settings, students can share their drafts and final versions with others, and adult leaders can provide further instruction and feedback based on the material in WIR.

A writing coach is any adult who wants to guide students through the material in WIR in an organized way—through an online class, by individualized tutoring, or in a co-op setting. Additional materials for co-ops and writing coaches are in development. You can sign up to receive notifications about the release date for these materials and future volumes in the WIR series at www.writers-in-residence.com.

Teaching Philosophy

The *Writers in Residence* series walks each student through the steps necessary to move from novice to expert writer—one who is confident and fascinated with the creative potential of language. To accomplish this, the following principles guide the teaching methods:

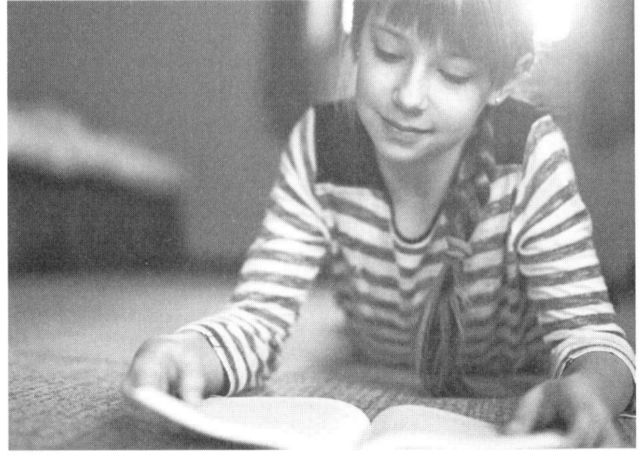

1. **Writing must be authentic.** Emerging writers should follow the same pathways professional writers have taken in the journey from beginner to experienced writer to expert writer. Assignments should mimic the writing activities and writing process adults engage in. Adults do not write to be graded. Rather, they write to inform, to influence, to entertain, and to understand themselves better. In the process the best writers solicit feedback from editors and readers so that their final creation is the best that it can be. These are the conditions and context that the *Writers in Residence* series seeks to simulate.

2. **Writing should be purposeful.** Writing tasks should be meaningful and interesting to students. Giving students a range of topics to write about and access to readers who are genuinely interested in what they have to say facilitates this goal. Parents, siblings, grandparents, friends, and writing groups may all be pressed into service as an audience for emerging writers.

3. **Writing is an apprenticeship.** Children master the English language by deep and long exposure to writers who have employed the creative potential of the written word for a wide variety of purposes. This means that writers must be readers—but not just casual readers. Students should learn to read closely and to notice what authors do to hold readers' interest, provoke their thinking, and focus their attention. Expert models from familiar authors and other experienced writers serve as a foundation for the writing tasks throughout WIR.

4. **Writing requires risk-taking and experimentation.** The world has no need for yet another high school composition written according to a prescribed form. What we need are those who can harness the power of language to craft narrative and argument that will shed new light on old mysteries. We need the unique, God-given voice of each child to be captured, polished, and shared. For this purpose, WIR creates a culture where students are rewarded for experimenting and taking risks. The emphasis is foremost on each student's ideas and unique voice. Students must be assured that progress, not perfection, is always the goal.

We need the unique, God-given voice of each child to be captured, polished, and shared.

5. **Writing is cyclical, repetitive, maddening, and inspired.** Writers must write to discover what they have to say. The process of writing is primed by the wellspring of inspiration, whose source is hidden who knows where! Writers ponder, write, retract, discuss, meditate, pray, rewrite, rethink, revise, stew, walk away, return, throw away, start again, eat chocolate, rewrite . . . and onward. The writing process is a discipline and a mystery. This is why it is so satisfying when writers finally get just the right words in just the right places. This means that students may write several versions of the same assignment or may change things substantially from one draft to another. This is a sign that they are on their way to becoming experts. Experts understand that good writing involves revising until their writing goals are achieved.

Writers ponder, write, retract, discuss, meditate, pray, rewrite, rethink, revise, stew, walk away, return, throw away, start again, eat chocolate, rewrite . . . and onward.

6. **Readers are paramount.** Students must never lose sight of the fact that written communication is intended to be read and understood. What we have to say must be relevant and meaningful for our readers. Therefore, writing is a humble endeavor—one where we always advocate for our readers by often considering how to compose our thoughts with greater grace, wit, and clarity.

WIR frequently reminds students that a writer's number one job is to keep readers reading.

Teaching Method

General Overview

I understand the time constraints of parents and teachers. You are multitasking all the time—probably juggling many children, many subjects, and many schedules simultaneously. While this program is student-centered and student-directed, it is designed with parents, teachers, and writing coaches in mind as well.

In particular, the introduction, rubric, and checklists in each unit are designed to help you quickly grasp the assignments and a student's progress. The *Answer Key and Teaching Notes* is also written so that you do not have to page back through the modules of the Student Text and Workbook in order to explain an answer.

Even so, please preview *Writers in Residence* before your student begins this program. This will give you a better framework for understanding the teaching approach and activities. It will also show you the trajectory I am following to build students' understanding about writing and the language arts.

Six Traits Writing Model

WIR uses a modified version of the six traits model for teaching and assessing writing. During the late 1970s and the early 1980s, several research teams asked writing teachers and college professors to identify the characteristics of good writing. Six distinct traits were mentioned over and over again in their answers. These six traits have been refined and applied in many classrooms and writing courses over the past two decades. The six traits are not new. They are just well defined and described in ways students seem to understand. For nearly two decades I have used the six traits model to teach students to write and evaluate their own writing. Since I adopted this paradigm, I find that students better understand how to improve their writing—and parents do too. The six traits approach takes the mystery out of teaching writing and provides the clarity we need to talk with our students about the strengths and weaknesses of the writing they produce.

The following six traits are used in WIR:

1. ideas
2. organization
3. sentence structure*
4. word choice
5. voice
6. conventions

*WIR uses sentence structure in place of sentence fluency. Later volumes of WIR will teach sentence fluency as a subset of sentence structure.

These traits are systematically introduced, explained, and practiced in the *Writers in Residence* series. No matter what type of writing a student is asked to produce, the final draft is evaluated using a rubric based on this six traits model. (A reproducible infographic designed to help students remember and apply the six traits of good writing appears on pages xxii–xxiii of the Student Text and Workbook.)

The Writing Process

The writing process is not always systematic or linear (see item 5 in the preceding section about teaching philosophy), but there are definite stages to the writing process:

1. planning
2. drafting
3. revising
4. editing
5. polishing

Expert writers accept that they must take a piece of writing through each of these stages multiple times before it is usable or publishable. WIR introduces students to these stages and gives them a toolbox of strategies to use at each point in the writing process.

The reproducible infographic on pages xxiv–xxv of the Student Text and Workbook attempts to show the cyclical and repetitive nature of the creative process. ("Two steps forward, one step back" might also be a helpful description.) Please keep this in mind as students struggle to gain expertise.

The Assignment Cycle

WIR cycles through four repeated types of writing tasks. All important forms of written expression can fit within this framework:

- **I Remember** writing assignments help students master the personal narrative.
- **I Imagine** assignments teach creative writing, such as short stories, poetry, and novels.
- **I Investigate** assignments teach students important research skills.
- **I Think** assignments teach opinion and argument writing, of which persuasive writing is a subset. (Argument writing is also known as academic writing.)

Language Arts

The conventions of the English language—grammar, punctuation, capitalization, spelling, formatting, and usage—are best taught in context. Students learn to value these conventions by using them to accomplish tasks that they care about. Learning conventions through this method requires much less time than the traditional method. You'll learn more about the WIR approach to grammar in the section on "Grammar Instruction" on pages 24–27 of this book.

Spelling

WIR does not teach spelling explicitly. Rather it asks students (and parents) to edit their work for spelling errors in the final stages. Accurate spelling is not essential for clear communication. Further, overemphasizing correct spelling often results in students using only words they are confident they can spell. This creates a boring and stilted writing style that is far below what the child is capable of thinking, imagining, and talking about. In the process, the child's voice is lost, not captured.

Overemphasizing correct spelling often results in students using only words they are confident they can spell. This creates a boring and stilted writing style that is far below what the child is capable of thinking, imagining, and talking about. In the process, the child's voice is lost, not captured.

To raise writers, we must create a learning culture where students are rewarded for expanding their vocabulary and experimenting with new words. To do this, spelling and usage mistakes should be tolerated, and attempts to try something new should be celebrated and encouraged.

In my experience, most students who write a lot for an audience achieve standardized spelling of common words by high school without separate instruction in this area. I suggest using a separate spelling program if the student asks for one or if the student repeatedly misspells a lot of common (not new) words and is not improving. Avoid using a program that is so time-consuming that students have little time left for real writing. Professional writers use a spell checker program to catch their spelling errors. In most cases, this is the best strategy for emerging writers as well.

The Role of a Parent, Teacher, or Writing Coach

The *Writers in Residence* series is designed for students to use independently, to the degree that is possible. Younger students and beginning writers need far more direct instruction and support from a parent, teacher, or writing coach than older, more experienced students. Greater independence will emerge as students gain greater control and mastery of the writing process.

However, meaningful written communication always presumes an audience; therefore, one of the greatest responsibilities of a parent, teacher, or writing coach is to provide that audience for the student. Without it, assignments are merely duties devoid of purpose. Writing must be authentic, and a student's time and efforts should be respected. What a child writes is a window into that child's intellectual life and development. Most of all, we should value the opportunity we have been given to share this process together.

What a child writes is a window into that child's intellectual life and development. Most of all, we should value the opportunity we have been given to share this process together.

Feedback

Targeted feedback is an essential support that parents, teachers, and writing coaches give to students. The Reviewer's Rubric for each writing assignment is designed to help you do this. It lists the key elements for each trait the student is asked to focus on in that assignment. Use the rubric as a basis for discussion and feedback.

Celebrate effort, progress, invention, and careful attention to the elements listed on the rubric.

Respond to a student's drafts as an interested reader. What ideas strike you as memorable or interesting? Talk about those first. What questions remain unanswered? Where would you like to know more? Approach sections that could be stronger from this angle. Notice new words a student uses, especially those collected from his or her reading or vocabulary lists. Celebrate effort, progress, invention, and careful attention to the elements listed on the rubric.

Occasionally, WIR encourages students to talk through their ideas with a parent, teacher, or writing coach. These are points where adult support and input are necessary. Talking through decision making as well as helping students understand the most important elements to focus on in a writing assignment will be critical to their success.

Grading

I strongly recommend that you not assign a letter grade to a writing assignment in this volume; rather evaluate each assignment for its strengths and weaknesses and for overall progress. The section on rubrics explains how to use this form of assessment. WIR includes unit reviews and mastery tests, which you can use for grading purposes if desired.

The Writer's Portfolio

Final drafts of the writing assignments should be compiled in one place: the Writer's Portfolio. Any additional writing projects from the year should also be included. The Writer's Portfolio might be posted online or kept in a computer folder or a three-ring binder. If possible, the child should decorate the portfolio, title it, and date it.

However the portfolio is configured, it should be designed to share with others. Children need a sense of accomplishment and a record of their progress. The Writer's Portfolio is a keepsake, an archive, and a powerful learning tool. As students review their polished written work from each school year, they will gain insight into their unique writing process, progress, and writer's voice.

The Writer's Portfolio is a keepsake, an archive, and a powerful learning tool. As students review their polished written work from each school year, they will gain insight into their unique writing process, progress, and writer's voice.

Grammar Instruction

English Grammar Defined

English grammar is the classification system we use to describe, explain, and analyze the basic units of speech used for written and oral communication. These basic units of speech are called grammatical units. (Grammatical units include parts of speech, phrases, clauses, and sentences.) Every domain from math to science to music has a method for organizing and classifying its fundamentals. It is the language we use to talk about a subject with others. We can't master a subject if we don't speak the language.

Grammar doesn't create content. But it can create beauty. English grammar provides the architecture for your child's ideas. And that's why it is important.

Grammar doesn't create content. But it can create beauty. English grammar provides the architecture for your child's ideas. And that's why it is important.

What Works

Here's what I've learned in thirty years of teaching kids how to write (and to love it).

- Kids can learn to follow the rules of English grammar without completing tedious exercises.
- Kids can learn how to use the fundamentals of English grammar to write better sentences. They can even find the process interesting. And it is okay if the adults in their lives are also learning more about English grammar right alongside them.

Here are a few things to keep in mind as you help your child with the grammar lessons in WIR:

1. Kids can't learn anything if they are not motivated. If students do not turn on their brains, focus their attention on the matter at hand, and choose to think deeply about the information, learning doesn't take place. (This truth explains why you don't remember a lot of things you supposedly learned in school. You weren't paying attention!)
2. It is easier to push a cart downhill than to pull it uphill. That's what momentum (or motivation) does. Parents and teachers need to use a downhill scenario, then, for teaching grammar. In the remainder of this section, I will show you just how to do that.
3. Grammar instruction is not an end in itself. There is no eternal value—and only a modest earthly one—in labeling and diagramming sentences. Grammar lessons should have practical value for the students, and each lesson must be linked to a real purpose that is immediate and relevant to their lives.

> Grammar instruction is not an end in itself.

4. Language arts (grammar, capitalization, punctuation, spelling, and usage) should be taught through practical application to writing tasks that kids care about. When students can study the conventions of English grammar in the writings of authors they admire, they have a sustaining interest and motivation to learn how to follow these rules. In fact, they will master the fundamentals of English grammar with increasing ease as the cycle of completing meaningful tasks and studying expert models is repeated.
5. The most powerful teaching method at your disposal is not in what you say, but in what you model. If you embrace the approach to grammar in the *Writers in Residence* series and show your kids that you find this information interesting and valuable, then they will get the message that English grammar is important to adult life.

The End Goal

Understanding the grammar of English won't produce original ideas or engaging content, but it will help students improve the structure and clarity of what they write. It will also help them analyze their sentences and identify sections that can be recast in more powerful ways. My goal is to teach young writers how grammatical units function so that they can engineer elegant, original sentences that have power and artistry.

The goal is to teach young writers how grammatical units function so that they can engineer elegant, original sentences that have power and artistry.

Grammar Focus in Volume 1

Volume 1 of this series introduces the parts of speech and shows students how each one can function in a sentence. The parts of speech introduced include nouns, verbs, adjectives, adverbs, conjunctions, prepositions, and interjections. (Pronouns are not covered in depth in volume 1; they are taught in volume 2.) Volume 1 also introduces the fundamentals of capitalization and punctuation.

Two other grammatical units are also included in volume 1: prepositional phrases and complements. Some parts of speech cannot be understood apart from the grammatical unit they are always included with. A preposition is always a part of a prepositional phrase, and a linking verb is always followed by a complement.

In addition to direct grammar instruction, WIR includes expert models that show students how accomplished writers use the grammatical units under discussion, as well as capitalization and punctuation, to create the stories we love.

By the end of volume 1, students should be able to analyze some of their own tendencies—both good and bad—in the sentences they build. Good writers are self-aware writers. They are their own best critics.

Grammar Focus in Volume 2

In volume 2, students start to use the language of English grammar to describe and discuss their writing. They learn more about the parts of speech included in volume 1 and are introduced to different types of pronouns, verb complements, points of view, and agreement among sentence parts. The standards for citing sources and using MLA formatting are also introduced.

Future Volumes

In future volumes students will learn about different types of phrases, clauses, and sentences. They will practice recognizing these in the expert models provided and will start to include them in their own writing assignments. Future volumes will also include advanced punctuation, capitalization, formatting skills, and in-depth study of verbs and tenses.

Finally, we will address style issues: parallel construction, coordination and subordination of ideas, shifts in subjects and tenses, wordiness, and redundancy. Throughout the series, students will study a wide variety of rich expert models from top-notch writers.

Why They'll Get It and Not Forget It

- Research shows that the students who frequently read and are read to, as well as those who write a lot, are most likely to use the conventions of the English language with the greatest accuracy and success.
- Intensive grammar study completed in isolation does not create better writers and readers.
- Exposure, not mastery, is the goal in the lower-level volumes of WIR. By returning to ideas and skills over and over again through unique and varied writing assignments, students will see how they can use what they learn.
- WIR uses a spiral approach to teaching concepts. A concept is introduced in one volume and expanded on as the series progresses. Information is not merely repeated; it is elaborated on and applied in new situations. Students' understanding of concepts will deepen and broaden over time when used in multiple situations.
- By the end of the series, students will have learned the content and skills presented in WIR through repeated, applied practice in a variety of contexts. Taught in this manner, they will not forget it.

In conclusion, have fun, learn alongside your kids, and push the cart downhill, not up!

Repeated Elements

Unit Introduction

The unit introduction provides an overview of the unit for both the student and the parent, teacher, or writing coach. It is designed as a reference tool to help you quickly grasp the writing assignment, focus of instruction, and language arts skills taught in the upcoming four modules.

Rubrics

A rubric is a special checklist for evaluating and grading writing or other projects. The rubric for each writing assignment focuses on the specific strategies and skills covered under each of the six traits of good writing in that unit. Students are held accountable only for what they have already learned and practiced. The focus is on progress, not perfection. All movement toward maturity in content and skill should be emphasized and celebrated.

Writers in Residence includes two types of rubrics. The **Student's Rubric** for the writing assignment appears in the unit introduction and again in the last module of the unit. With the help of a parent, teacher, or writing coach, students evaluate their finished assignments with the rubric. The points earned on the Student's Rubric are filled in on the Journeyman Log.

Parents, teachers, and other readers can use a **Reviewer's Rubric**, provided in the appendix of the Student Text and Workbook and in the back of this book. The Reviewer's Rubric is designed to help readers give students targeted feedback. Reviewer's Rubrics should be used in the context of conversation with students, as some items will be impossible to perceive based on the writing sample alone. The points on the Reviewer's Rubric are not filled in on the Journeyman Log.

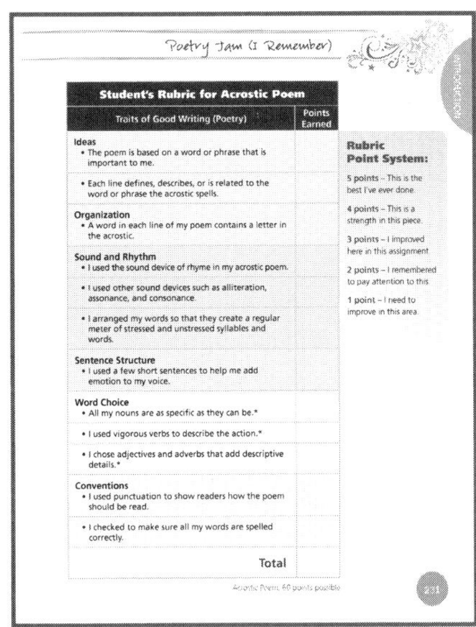

Poetry Jam (I Remember)

Student's Rubric for Acrostic Poem

Traits of Good Writing (Poetry)	Points Earned
Ideas • The poem is based on a word or phrase that is important to me.	
• Each line defines, describes, or is related to the word or phrase the acrostic spells.	
Organization • A word in each line of my poem contains a letter in the acrostic.	
Sound and Rhythm • I used the sound device of rhyme in my acrostic poem.	
• I used other sound devices such as alliteration, assonance, and consonance.	
• I arranged my words so that they create a regular meter of stressed and unstressed syllables and words.	
Sentence Structure • I used a few short sentences to help me add emotion to my voice.	
Word Choice • All my nouns are as specific as they can be.*	
• I used vigorous verbs to describe the action.*	
• I chose adjectives and adverbs that add descriptive details.*	
Conventions • I used punctuation to show readers how the poem should be read.	
• I checked to make sure all my words are spelled correctly.	
Total	

Acrostic Poem, 60 points possible

Rubric Point System:

5 points – This is the best I've ever done.

4 points – This is a strength in this piece.

3 points – I improved here in this assignment.

2 points – I remembered to pay attention to this.

1 point – I need to improve in this area.

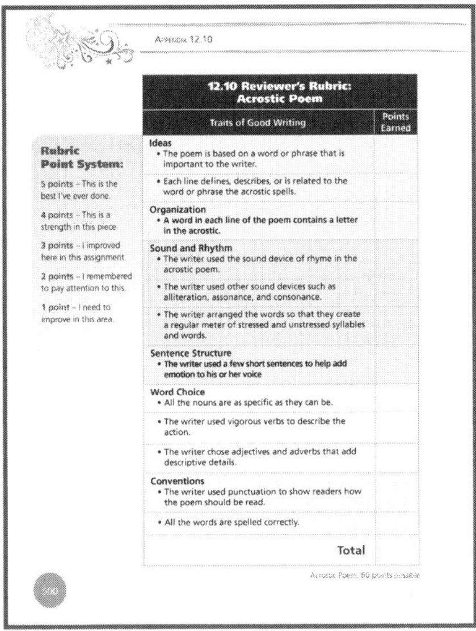

Appendix 12.10

12.10 Reviewer's Rubric: Acrostic Poem

Traits of Good Writing	Points Earned
Ideas • The poem is based on a word or phrase that is important to the writer.	
• Each line defines, describes, or is related to the word or phrase the acrostic spells.	
Organization • **A word in each line of the poem contains a letter in the acrostic.**	
Sound and Rhythm • The writer used the sound device of rhyme in the acrostic poem.	
• The writer used other sound devices such as alliteration, assonance, and consonance.	
• The writer arranged the words so that they create a regular meter of stressed and unstressed syllables and words.	
Sentence Structure • **The writer used a few short sentences to help add emotion to his or her voice**	
Word Choice • All the nouns are as specific as they can be.	
• The writer used vigorous verbs to describe the action.	
• The writer chose adjectives and adverbs that add descriptive details.	
Conventions • The writer used punctuation to show readers how the poem should be read.	
• All the words are spelled correctly.	
Total	

Acrostic Poem, 60 points possible

Rubric Point System:

5 points – This is the best I've ever done.

4 points – This is a strength in this piece.

3 points – I improved here in this assignment.

2 points – I remembered to pay attention to this.

1 point – I need to improve in this area.

Writer's Questions

At the beginning of each module, the Writer's Questions remind students to turn on their brains and get ready to learn. Students should hold these questions in mind as they work through the module to gain experience and expertise. At the end of each module, students will discuss their answers to these questions with a parent, teacher, or writing coach. This activity will reinforce their understanding and retention of the most important information in that module.

Writer's Questions

What is poetry?

How do I create sound in my poems?

How do I show but not tell readers how I feel about the subjects of my poems?

Sneak Peek

This section at the beginning of each module provides a preview of the primary skills and concepts to be practiced and incorporated into the writing assignment. These objectives also provide insight into possible answers to the writer's questions.

Sneak Peek

In this module you will learn:

- Poetry shows the beauty and power of language.
- Poetry is created through sound, rhythm, and meaning.
- Poets use vigorous verbs, specific nouns, and descriptive modifiers to create vivid imagery in their readers' minds.

The Assignment

The writing assignment at the beginning of each module identifies the key areas students will focus on as they work through the unit.

Expert Model

Each unit includes one or more pieces of writing by an expert writer—often a familiar author. Students learn to analyze these models and to note the specific strategies the expert used to accomplish the goal of the writing task.

EXPERT MODEL

The Eagle
By Alfred, Lord Tennyson

He clasps the crag with crooked hands;
Close to the sun in lonely lands,
Ring'd with the azure world, he stands.

The wrinkled sea beneath him crawls;
He watches from his mountain walls,
And like a thunderbolt he falls.

Student Samples

Samples of student work show students how to complete writing activities.

Writer's Toolbox

Throughout WIR, specific strategies that expert writers use are set apart in the Writer's Toolbox. The appendix of the Student Text and Workbook includes a list of these strategies in an attractive, reproducible form for easy reference.

Graphic Organizers

WIR uses graphic organizers to help students generate ideas and organize their content. Graphic organizers are more powerful teaching tools than formal outlining because they help students visualize their projects and identify the relationships among the parts of their essays and stories.

Comparison Chart of Possible Destinations				
Destination				
Costs				
Distance				
Activities				
Other Details				

The Sandbox

The Sandbox sections of WIR give students a place to experiment with various writing strategies. They also give students a break from the longer writing task of the unit. Student writing improves when students write a lot. The Sandbox is one way to keep students composing. Space for completing the Sandbox assignments is not included in the Student Text and Workbook. These are to be handwritten on the student's own paper or typed on a computer.

Word Sleuth

In volume 1, students are asked to collect new words they want to remember to use and words they realize they are prone to misspell. In volume 2, the Word Sleuth sections continue to spark students' interest and attention to new words with a variety of assignments that draw on their reading, imagination, and research. Furthermore, many terms in the text of WIR are defined in the glossary at the back of the book; these words are highlighted in the lesson text. Vocabulary is more heavily emphasized in the companion program, *Readers in Residence*, where students see vocabulary words used in context. This is the key way all of us—including students—learn what words mean and how they can be used.

Module Checklist

A checklist at the end of each module serves a twofold purpose: It helps students keep track of their progress and gives parents, teachers, and writing coaches a quick way to make sure students have fully completed all the assigned work in each module. The point system is a method of evaluation that emphasizes progress rather than grading. The student checks off the work he or she has completed. The parent, teacher, or writing coach awards points based on the point system provided.

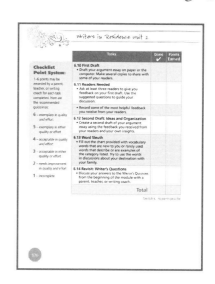

Writer's Workshop

The sentence is the fundamental organizational unit for composing thought in the modern English language. (You can find the interesting history of the sentence online if you are so inclined.) Emerging writers need the most practice at the sentence level. In most units in this series, one module specifically focuses on sentence structure. In volume 1 of WIR, students review the parts of speech and practice using them. Students then create and revise sentences in the module and in their writing assignment, focusing on this sentence part.

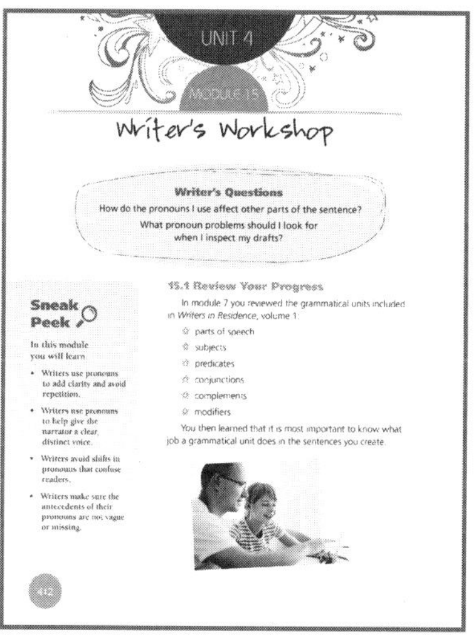

UNIT 4

MODULE 15

Writer's Workshop

Writer's Questions

How do the pronouns I use affect other parts of the sentence?

What pronoun problems should I look for when I inspect my drafts?

Sneak Peek

In this module you will learn:

- Writers use pronouns to add clarity and avoid repetition.
- Writers use pronouns to help give the narrator a clear, distinct voice.
- Writers avoid shifts in pronouns that confuse readers.
- Writers make sure the antecedents of their pronouns are not vague or missing.

15.1 Review Your Progress

In module 7 you reviewed the grammatical units included in *Writers in Residence*, volume 1:

- parts of speech
- subjects
- predicates
- conjunctions
- complements
- modifiers

You then learned that it is most important to know what job a grammatical unit does in the sentences you create.

412

In volume 2 of WIR, the Writer's Workshop covers MLA formatting, verb complements (including direct and indirect objects), pronouns, point of view, and agreement.

In subsequent volumes, students progress from learning the basic parts of speech to learning how to use phrases and clauses to build more complex sentences. Proper punctuation is taught concurrently with learning how to compose different types of sentences. The Writer's Workshop sections of WIR are marked with an orange tab to help you find them easily.

Review Your Progress

Systematic review of concepts and skills is integrated throughout WIR. Explicit review is provided through "Review Your Progress" sections, mastery tests, and unit reviews. A cumulative assessment in the form of a Final Review is provided at the end of each volume. However, these assessments are intended to be used as teaching tools rather than grading instruments. Allow students to review their writing and the relevant modules while composing their answers. Encourage students to talk about their responses with a parent, teacher, or writing coach before finalizing their answers to the review questions.

Unit Review

The unit review asks students to demonstrate their understanding of the writing concepts and strategies taught in the entire unit.

Mastery Test

A mastery test appears at the end of some Writer's Workshop modules. It reviews conventions of the English language and grammar terms.

Final Review

At the end of each volume is a final review designed to reinforce and deepen students' understanding of the concepts and skills covered in that volume. Students are also asked to reflect about the writing projects they produced that term. This is an important step in helping young writers learn to constructively evaluate what they produce so they can learn to improve. A parent, teacher, or writing coach should participate in this process. However, the focus should be on what the student thinks, so he or she should do most of the talking.

Journeyman Log

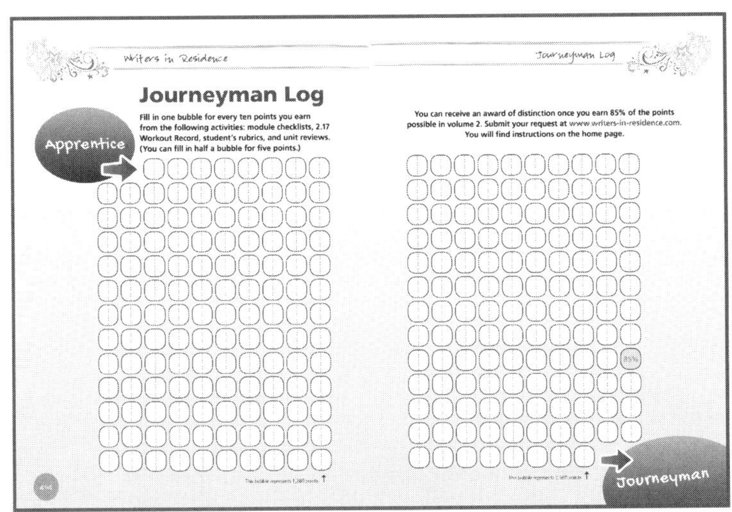

A Journeyman Log in the appendix of the Student Text and Workbook provides a place for students to fill in the total points they earn on the following activities in WIR:

- module checklists
- workout record (2.17)
- student's rubrics
- unit reviews

Students can earn an award of distinction if they earn 85% of the points possible in volume 2. Submit your request to receive your award of distinction at **www.writers-in-residence.com**. You will find instructions on the home page.

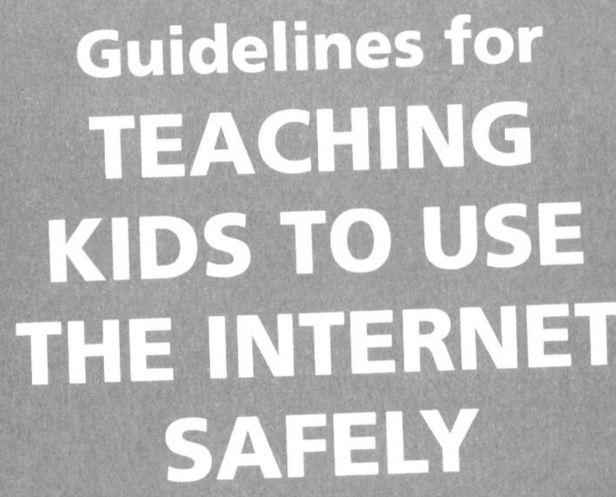

Guidelines for TEACHING KIDS TO USE THE INTERNET SAFELY

By Leah Nieman
leahnieman.com

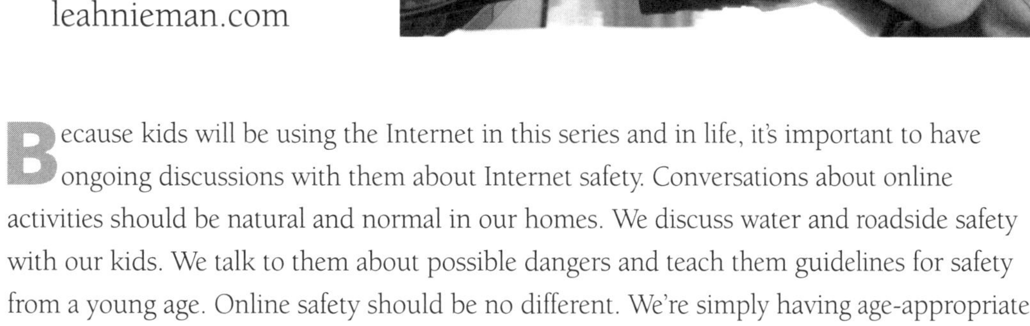

Because kids will be using the Internet in this series and in life, it's important to have ongoing discussions with them about Internet safety. Conversations about online activities should be natural and normal in our homes. We discuss water and roadside safety with our kids. We talk to them about possible dangers and teach them guidelines for safety from a young age. Online safety should be no different. We're simply having age-appropriate discussions with our kids so that they become adults who are digitally responsible.

Here are a few guidelines:

1. Have a family digital media agreement.
   As the old adage says, "If you fail to plan, you are planning to fail." This statement is so true when it comes to online safety. Communication is key! Most families struggle with technology because they don't have a plan for it. Having a family digital media agreement gives everyone in your home guidelines for Internet usage. You can find a digital media agreement that you can download and use with your family on the Book Extras website at www.apologia.com/bookextras. Please use the password—godcreatedlanguage—to access the *Writers in Residence* page.

2. Teach kids to carefully check the URL before clicking through to a website.
   Most legitimate websites' URLs end in *.com*, *.org*, *.edu*, or *.gov*. Page 27 in the Student Text and Workbook has a detailed listing of domain name extensions for reference. If you start seeing additional extensions after the *.com*, *.org*, *.edu*, or *.gov* or see anything that is not a normal URL ending, you should question the source.

3. **Teach kids to shut off the monitor and get a parent.**
   Teach your children that if they see inappropriate, scary, or upsetting websites or images, they need to shut off the monitor and immediately get a parent. This enables the child to block the image but does not shut off the computer. You'll then be able to hit the ON button to look at the screen and find out why your child is upset. Be sure to discuss the website or image with your child as well. This will give you the opportunity to help your child process the content he saw. It will also provide valuable information so that you can prevent the site from getting through your filter in the future. Make any necessary changes to your filter.

4. **Stay calm.**
   Kids make mistakes, and accidents happen. Often, kids don't tell their parents when something bad happens online because they fear punishment. It's hard to keep kids safe and guide them when you aren't aware of what's happening. That's why it's important to stay calm if your child comes to you for help with Internet issues. Assure kids they are safe by thanking them for their honesty when they talk to you. Take a moment to evaluate the situation. Then come back with a solution and guidance if needed. In the end, this will help keep open lines of communication with your child. And that's the goal!

5. **Use an Internet filter and kid-friendly search engine.**
   Make sure your browser is set to filter out explicit content. Also, when searching for images, use an advanced search to limit the results to images that can be used free of charge. In addition, use one of the recommended Internet filters and a kid-friendly search engine. Keep in mind that there is no guarantee against offensive material, but these suggestions will go a long way toward blocking it out.

Recommended Internet Filters

Koala Safe
https://koalasafe.com

Covenant Eyes
http://www.covenanteyes.com

Net Nanny
https://www.netnanny.com

Kid-Friendly Search Engines

KidRex

KidRex uses a combination of Google Safe Search and Google Custom Search.

Google Safe Search	Google Custom Search
Google Safe Search screens keywords, phrases, and URLs from search results.	KidRex has added its own list of inappropriate websites. These sites are blocked and won't get pulled in a search using KidRex.

KidRex also has a webpage removal request tool so that users can report websites that need to be added to the list of inappropriate websites.

KidsSearch

KidsSearch is designed to be used by libraries and schools. It's also perfect for home use. This is a valuable search engine for researching topics. My favorite feature of KidsSearch is that kids can easily search by what they want to find: web, pictures, videos, games, and more.

Google Safe Search	Google Custom Search
Google Safe Search screens keywords, phrases, and URLs from search results.	KidsSearch screens outbound links using filters in addition to using Google Safe Search.

KidsSearch uses feedback from the community. If you find a bad or inappropriate link, simply report it.

KidsClick

KidsClick is owned and operated by the School of Library and Information Science at Kent University. KidsClick is not a filter. It does not prevent users from being able to access any URL address that they enter. KidsClick is intended to guide users to good sites, not block them from bad sites.

Anyone can read KidsClick's selection criteria for websites. I love that they don't allow websites with unsafe privacy features for kids or sites that require an access fee.

Teaching Notes

Listed below are the important concepts covered in *Writers in Residence*, volume 2. (This chart also appears in the Student Text and Workbook, Final Review, page 476.) The chart is included here as a preview for parents, teachers, and writing coaches. Students are asked to discuss what they have learned about each concept with you during the Final Review.

Important Concepts			
readers	essay	conclusion	rhythm
rubric	logical reasons	grammatical units	mood
reliable source	facts	parts of speech	lyric poetry
verifiable source	apt examples	subject	haiku
Internet research	details	predicate	poetic license
library research	data	modifier	connotation
choosing a topic	six traits of good writing	connector	figures of speech
study strategies	ideas	complement	allusion
plagiarism	organization	types of verbs	punctuation
in-text citation	sentence structure	function words	writing process
bibliography	word choice	types of pronouns	feedback
MLA style	conventions	antecedent	inspect and improve
paraphrase	voice	agreement	setting
summarize	tone	point of view	characterization
interrogative	thesis	poetry	plot
interviewing skills	topic sentence	imagery	narrator
argument	introduction	sound	show but don't tell

Unit 1

This chart lists activities where students are instructed to ask a parent, teacher, or writing coach to assist them.

Unit 1			
Plan Ahead (page 8)	1.16 Word Sleuth	2.18 Find an Expert	Checklist 3
1.4 Get Your Gear	1.17 Revisit: Writer's Questions	2.19 Take Your Field Trip	4.6 The Order Matters
1.7 Test 1: Who Said It?	Checklist 1	2.21 Revisit: Writer's Questions	4.7 Illustrate Your Science Report
1.9 Internet Research	2.4 Library Research	Checklist 2	4.8 Readers Needed
1.10 Types of Websites	2.6 Research the Resources	3.7 Conventions: Titles	4.11 You Be the Judge
1.11 Test Drive	2.7 Is It Reliable? Is It Verifiable?	3.10 Paraphrase	4.13 Revisit: Writer's Questions
1.13 Investigate This	2.8 And the Winner Is . . .	3.11 Summarize	Checklist 4
1.14 Where the Wild Things Are	2.14 Study Strategy 5: Learn New Words in Context	3.14 Revisit: Writer's Questions	Unit 1 Review

"Into the Wild" (I Investigate)

The primary purpose of the "I Investigate" units is to teach students how to do research writing. This type of writing is very important for their academic success, especially if students are college bound. It also fosters cognitive development. Research writing requires a sophisticated set of skills; students will need a lot of practice to develop these.

This unit is an introduction to the fundamentals of academic research:

- choosing a good topic to research
- finding reliable and verifiable information
- using the Internet safely
- gathering resources from the library
- properly crediting the sources used in the report

Because researching a topic to write about is a lengthy process, I chose a simple way for students to organize their research: Q&A format. Later assignments in the *Writers in Residence* series will focus on writing a research paper—including synthesizing the research of others with their own voice and analysis. Before we get to that, though, students need to learn how to find good sources of information about a topic and study those sources thoroughly before writing the paper. (In my experience, few students put adequate time into this step.)

You may wonder why I call the finished assignment a science report, not a research paper. A report paraphrases and summarizes factual information in the author's own words. A true research paper contains a thesis and the author's original ideas and analysis. That's where we will head in volumes 3 and 4 of this series.

Plan Ahead

A field trip is a requirement for this assignment. I realize this may be a challenge for you to arrange, but it will be well worth the effort. Firsthand experience is a critical source of information for writers. Over the years I've found that students produce their best writing about their experiences. Later volumes will emphasize adding their own voice and insights to their research papers; firsthand experience with the topics they write about will be the most likely source of that originality. So I hope you can make this activity happen.

Students are also asked to visit the library to collect resources for this assignment. This is scheduled for 2.5–2.7 on the Suggested Daily Schedule.

Choosing a Topic

Most unsuccessful writing projects begin with a poorly considered topic. That is why I ask students to spend a lot of time researching possible topics for the assignments in this volume. If your child doesn't struggle with this issue, then feel free to streamline this process. In later volumes of *Writers in Residence*, I will not require this much effort. I break down the process here into explicit steps in the hope that students will automatically cycle through this process (at least mentally) before committing to a topic in future assignments.

Internet Research

In the *Writers in Residence* series, I will always tell students to ask a parent, teacher, or writing coach to help them when they are required to use the Internet for research. This is to help you monitor their online use. The Internet is a rich source of valuable information for research writers, but it is also fraught with peril, especially for children. I found that teaching my own kids to use the Internet safely was akin to teaching them to drive—they had a lot to learn, and they needed a lot of practice with my husband or me beside them (stomping on the imaginary brakes!). I view students as having their learners' permits in this series. They will need your help for Internet-related activities.

You will find guidelines for using the Internet safely in the Student Text and Workbook on pages 26–27. Additional information for parents is provided on pages 33–35 of this book. Please preview this information and be available to help your child with the Internet activities.

Wikipedia

Wikipedia represents an evolving source of information. At this time, it is not broadly accepted as a reliable source of information for academic papers. Wikipedia entries have no attributed authorship because the information is crowdsourced. That means that many people have contributed to the page—some who have professional credentials and many who do not. Further complicating this issue is Wikipedia's policy of allowing people to post anonymously. Despite this, early research has found that many Wikipedia entries are comparable in accuracy to printed encyclopedia entries. Other studies have found that most errors are corrected within minutes. Advocates note that print sources of information go out of date quickly, while Wikipedia entries reflect the most current information. Because of this, the acceptability of Wikipedia as a source in academic contexts is growing. However, its reliability is still significantly uncertain, so it is not a recommended source for this series.

In my online high school classes, I allowed students to use Wikipedia as an initial source of information but not as a source for their citations or bibliographic entries. Instead, I showed them how to use the footnotes at the bottom of a Wikipedia entry to track down a more reliable and verifiable source that they could then use in their research papers. This may be an option you consider for older students. I don't recommend Wikipedia as a source for elementary or middle school students—the entries are not well written or engaging.

Please note that Wikipedia entries often turn up at the top of an Internet search, so please discuss the issues surrounding this source as you help your child learn to conduct online research for this unit.

Library Research

While Internet research may seem more convenient, your local public library is still your best resource for reliable and verifiable information. How libraries catalogue their collections, though, is in flux. Some are moving away from the Dewey Decimal System in favor of a word-based system with categories and subcategories, similar to what bookstores use. Most libraries require users to know how to search a database to find the resources that are available (as opposed to the out-of-date card catalog). Because of the evolving nature of our library systems, I elected not to teach how to use the Dewey Decimal System in this series. Rather, I hope you will take advantage of the training your local library provides. Students will be asked to use the library in future research assignments.

If you are not already familiar with your local library, you may want to make a trip before you begin this unit. Some books that your child will need for this project may need to be placed on reserve or requested through the interlibrary loan system.

MLA Style

This unit introduces students to the Modern Language Association's (MLA) conventions for formatting a research paper and citing sources. Students are often not required to adhere to these standards prior to middle school. I introduce them here because the *Writers in Residence* series is used by a wide age range of students. If this is your child's first experience with citing sources and preparing a bibliography, feel free to modify these requirements to match your child's readiness.

The *Writers in Residence* series uses the MLA Handbook, 8th edition (ISBN: 978-1603292627). This is a major update, so it will differ from the conventions you followed in school. The *MLA Style Center: Writing Resources from the Modern Language Association* is a thorough and helpful website you may wish to consult (style.mla.org).

Even though the *Chicago Manual of Style* is followed in the book publishing industry (and is used in most Apologia books) for parenthetical citations and works cited, we have adopted MLA style for this series, starting with volume 2, so that students will not be confused by two different systems. The Works Cited list in the Student Text and Workbook (pages 489–491) reflects MLA formatting, so students can use this as an expert model as well.

Plagiarism

In thirty years as an English teacher, I have had my share of encounters with plagiarism. But this has shown me that I have an important obligation to my students: I must provide plenty of instruction to help them. I am deeply committed to addressing that obligation in this series.

Most young students commit plagiarism for several reasons:

1. They don't know what plagiarism is.
2. They don't know any strategies for avoiding it.
3. They don't know enough about the topic they are writing about to put information into their own words.

Avoiding plagiarism requires sophisticated writing skills. Not only must students learn how to paraphrase and summarize in their own words, but they must also learn a variety of sentence patterns to use (since it is also plagiarism to use the same sentence structure as the original author, only changing a word or two). Students need time and practice to learn how to do all these things. I will continue to provide instruction about plagiarism in this series and give kids plenty of opportunity to practice avoiding it. I encourage parents, teachers, and writing coaches to be patient and supportive as students learn these skills. Most students will need your help incorporating what others have written into their papers.

A good strategy to help students transform what they have read into their own words is to ask them to tell you what they have learned. Take notes for them as they talk, and then let them use your notes as a first draft for what they write. You will find helpful information about plagiarism at this website: plagiarism.org.

Paraphrasing and Summarizing

These important skills are introduced in this unit. They are both advanced writing skills. Don't be surprised if students struggle with the activities on pages 88–92. They may need a lot of assistance from you. By the end of this series, students will feel confident in their ability to paraphrase and summarize. As with many concepts and skills taught in *Writers in Residence* series, paraphrasing and summarizing are also taught in the *Readers in Residence* series. (It is a bit easier to show students how to paraphrase and summarize when studying a book together.)

Unit 2

This chart lists activities where students are instructed to ask a parent, teacher, or writing coach to assist them.

Unit 2			
5.10 Interview the Experienced	6.11 Readers Needed	7.12 Revisit: Writer's Questions	8.14 With Fanfare and Panache
5.11 Search and Verify	6.14 Revisit: Writer's Questions	Checklist 7	8.16 You Be the Judge
5.14 Revisit: Writer's Questions	Checklist 6	8.5 Voice: Show Your Emotions	8.18 Revisit: Writer's Questions
Checklist 5	7.3 Quick Review	8.8 Inspect and Improve: Sentence Structure	Checklist 8
6.7 Body Paragraphs: Organization Again	7.11 Word Sleuth	8.12 Inspect and Improve: Conventions	Unit 2 Review

"Making the Case" (I Think)

The primary purpose of the "I Think" units is to teach students argument writing. (This is sometimes called academic writing.) This unit intentionally follows the "I Investigate" unit because solid arguments begin with solid research. All the skills covered in unit 1 will be put to good use again. If students completed *Writers in Residence*, volume 1, then they were introduced to argument writing in unit 4, "My Favorite Author." If so, consider reviewing that unit with them, as well as the final version of the personal essay they created for that assignment. This review will trigger memories and also provide additional examples for students to keep in mind.

Argument writing is one of the most powerful learning experiences you can provide for your children. Formulating opinions about what they experience and read and then supporting those opinions with logical reasons based on facts, apt examples, and descriptive details is one way kids learn to think deeply about important issues. Many students may find the first two units in this volume stretching. However, the skills taught will not only help them become better writers; they will also help your kids become better learners in all their subjects.

Plan Ahead

In 5.10 Interview the Experienced, students are asked to schedule interviews with at least two people who have firsthand experience planning a vacation. The interviewees can include you or another family member, a travel agent, or a family friend.

More Research Skills

This unit adds to the research skills students learned in unit 1. Students are introduced to some of the important skills of scientific research—survey construction, data collection, and data analysis. Are you surprised to find this in an English program? Scientific research is fundamental to formulating opinions based on logical reasons and solid evidence. To be ready for college by the end of high school, students should know how to be systematic thinkers; collecting evidence is a critical part of this process.

Learning how to do original research will also help your child avoid plagiarism. Original research makes it much easier for students to combine their own voice and analysis with information written by others. As I noted earlier, students often plagiarize because they don't know enough about the topics they write about. Original research is one way to avoid this problem.

The student's original research for this unit will come from the activities in 5.6–5.8 and 5.10.

Essay Writing

This unit continues to build students' essay writing skills. The essay is the form of writing most often used for expressing an opinion, especially in an academic setting. An essay includes an introduction, body paragraphs, and a conclusion. Each of these has a specific job to do. In WIR volume 2, the expert model of an essay is annotated to show students how each sentence in each paragraph of the essay fulfills a specific function. Students should know exactly what job every sentence in an essay is intended to accomplish. During your discussions with students about their drafts, ask them to talk to you about each sentence and the type of information they are attempting to include in it. This will help them grow as self-aware writers who are capable of analyzing their strengths and weaknesses as they compose. This self-awareness will eventually help students gain control of their writing processes.

The expert model is annotated on pages 126–128 and again on pages 157–159 of the Student Text and Workbook. You have permission to photocopy the expert model so that students can keep it in front of them as they work through this unit.

Thesis

The most important component of an argument essay is the thesis. The thesis states the position that the writer will argue in the essay. It contains an opinion that can be supported with logical reasoning, facts, and examples. In my experience students need a lot of help and practice before they learn to write a solid thesis on their own. Some common problems I have seen include the following:

- The thesis doesn't contain an opinion.
- The thesis contains an opinion that is not arguable. For example, the student's opinion is closer to a statement of fact.
- The thesis doesn't contain an opinion that is broad enough to develop into a multiparagraph essay.
- The thesis cannot be supported with logical reasoning, facts, or examples. The thesis may be too emotionally charged. It may be based only on personal experience. Or the student just doesn't have the time to do the research necessary to back up his or her claims.
- The thesis is too broad to be successfully defended in just a few paragraphs. In this case, students have chosen a complex issue with too many facets that must be considered. If a student is committed to the topic, help him or her narrow it down to just one aspect of the issue.

Even if your student develops a thesis with these types of problems, it is fine to let him or her try to develop an argument essay based on it. Kids learn by doing. In later volumes of *Writers in Residence*, we will continue to look at thesis development in depth. The rule of thumb here is to use your judgment when deciding how much effort to require of your child when tackling the activities in this series. At the end of the day, kids need to feel successful throughout their journey from novice to expert writer.

Six Traits of Good Writing

I use this unit to show students how the six traits of good writing can be applied to their essays. My goal is to make students highly aware of the six traits and to train them to evaluate what they write in light of each trait, one at a time. Experienced writers draft and revise while holding all six traits (and more) fully in mind simultaneously. Looking at each one individually in this unit and revising accordingly may seem unnecessary for some students, but please assure them that we will move on to a more holistic approach in later volumes. Right now, the six traits are the training wheels that will take students to more sophisticated writing in the future.

Writer's Workshop

This unit's Writer's Workshop returns to teaching the fundamental sentence parts that writers use to build strong sentences. In this volume, I introduce the technical term for these parts—grammatical units. (In volume 1, I just called them sentence parts.) Depending on how much grammar instruction your student has had prior to using *Writers in Residence*, these modules may be merely a review, or they may seem like an introduction to a foreign language (and be completely overwhelming). Please adjust the amount of help you give your kids with these modules accordingly. If your goal is to help your kids learn to write at the highest levels of their ability, then they need to understand the function of the grammatical units that writers use to build sentences. In volumes 3 and 4, students will learn the common sentence patterns writers build with these grammatical units. (So stick with me—we are getting ready to start a major construction zone with these tools.)

The content in the Writer's Workshops will always be reviewed and built on, so it is just fine if kids do not completely master the information in these modules. The most important concept in the Writer's Workshops in this volume is on page 176, 7.4 It's What It Does That Matters. If student writers can remember that every part of their sentences is doing one of only five possible jobs, then I will be able to show them how to write stronger, clearer sentences in the forthcoming volumes.

Unit 3

This chart lists activities where students are instructed to ask a parent, teacher, or writing coach to assist them.

Unit 3		
9.3 What Makes a Poem a Poem?	Checklist 10	12.12 Poetry Jam
9.15 Revisit: Writer's Questions	11.9 Point of View	12.13 You Be the Judge
Checklist 9	11.12 Revisit: Writer's Questions	12.15 Revisit: Writer's Questions
10.6 Revise for Sound and Rhythm	Checklist 11	Checklist 12
10.10 Revisit: Writer's Questions	12.4 Denotations and Connotations of Words	Unit 3 Review

"Poetry Jam" (I Remember)

It's time for a whole new direction. While units 1 and 2 emphasized analytical writing, the last two units give kids the opportunity to develop their creative writing skills. The "I Remember" units focus on writing assignments drawn from a student's memories and experiences. These assignments are personal and do not generally require outside reading or research. Most kids will find these assignments less time consuming than research or argument writing—and many will find them more enjoyable. (Don't hesitate to remind them, though, that breaking a cognitive sweat is helping their brains to grow.)

Poetry is an acquired taste for most of us. I assume students have not had much of an introduction to poetry, so before they write their first poems, I spend a lot of time showing them the characteristics that distinguish poetry from prose. If your student is not ready to fully understand some of the technical aspects of poetry, please don't overemphasize this information. Playing with language is the main goal I hope to accomplish with the assignments in this unit. I plan to return to poetry again in the *Writers in Residence* series, and *Readers in Residence* will also include a poetry collection.

The Poems They Write

Students are asked to create an acrostic, a lyric poem, a haiku, and a cinquain in this unit. The acrostic, haiku, and cinquain are short poems. I want students to really work on every single word they select for these assignments. I hope that working with shorter poems will help them be willing to do this. The lyric poem will likely be the most challenging to write because so much has to be accomplished in it. Please communicate to your child the value of tinkering with each poem *a lot*. In my experience, students are

quickly satisfied with the poems they create, and I had to become a master motivator to get them to keep revising. (Good luck! I'm rooting for you.)

If possible, combine reading or listening to poetry with this unit. Another suggestion is to talk about the lyrics of songs your family enjoys. Many songs, especially hymns and worship songs, have poetic qualities.

Pronouns

I did not cover pronouns in *Writers in Residence*, volume 1, because I wanted to use them in this volume to teach students how to write from a consistent point of view. I hope this meaningful context will help students pay closer attention to the pronouns they use as they write. Many fundamental grammatical and stylistic errors in student writing involve pronouns. For this reason, I will return to pronouns often, including the Writer's Workshop for unit 4.

Notice that I introduce the concept of function words versus content words in the unit 3 Writer's Workshop. If you have time, please discuss these terms with your students. It is helpful for students to be able to divide the parts of speech into these two categories.

Point of View

Point of view, like voice and tone, is a very advanced concept for students to grasp. They will likely find that identifying first-person, second-person, and third-person pronouns is simple enough. But understanding how pronouns establish the point of view is another matter. I introduce point of view in the poetry unit and continue to develop the concept and its use in unit 4, where students write a short story. They may find establishing a consistent point of view easier in unit 4 than in their poems.

The Sandbox

The Sandbox is a place for students to mess around with engaging writing activities that they are not required to revise and polish. It's a break from the effort and rigor required for the major unit assignments. However, if students become deeply involved with a Sandbox activity, don't hesitate to adapt the unit to allow them to take this prompt through the full writing process. In this unit in particular, students could replace one of the other poetry assignments with their humorous poem.

Figures of Speech

The English language includes dozens of figures of speech. Metaphor and simile are just two of them. Many lists also categorize allusions as figures of speech (though not all authoritative sources do). All three are presented in this unit. Figures of speech are a major focus in this language arts curriculum (particularly in *Readers in Residence*) because students' reading comprehension is significantly affected by their understanding of them. In general, figures of speech are words and phrases that are not intended to be taken literally. You can see the problems that can arise if students don't understand this or if they do not know what the words and phrases actually mean. (For example, consider the possible confusion that can arise from an idiom like "It's raining cats and dogs" or "You're barking up the wrong tree.")

Even though recognizing figures of speech and their intended meanings most significantly affects reading comprehension, students can understand them better if they use them in their own writing (because they know what meaning they intend to get across). Figures of speech also add layers of meaning, which are particularly important in poetry.

Unit 4

This chart lists activities where students are instructed to ask a parent, teacher, or writing coach to assist them.

Unit 4			
Plan Ahead (page 354)	14.10 Revisit: Writer's Questions	15.11 Revisit: Writer's Questions	16.11 Finally, Final Draft
13.2 Why Imagine?	Checklist 14	Checklist 15	16.12 You Be the Judge
13.11 Revisit: Writer's Questions	15.4 Reflexive Pronouns	16.4 Recruit Some Expert Readers	16.14 Revisit: Writer's Questions
Checklist 13	15.9 Inspect and Improve: Pronouns	16.8 Show but Don't Tell	Checklist 16
14.5 Third-Person Point of View	15.10 Word Sleuth	16.9 Vivify Your Voices	Unit 4 Review

Students will also need your assistance for the Final Review on pages 475–477.

"A Fantastical Tale of Extraordinary Exploits" (I Imagine)

The "I Imagine" units are designed to teach students the primary aspects of creative writing. My secondary intention is to show students how fiction works so that they will better understand the literature they study. In this unit, students learn how to develop the primary components of a short story. Most of these were studied in depth in *Readers in Residence*, volume 1. If you did not use that program, students will still be able to complete this project with the instructional content I provide here. (But using both programs provides students with a lot of synergy.)

Plan Ahead

On pages 365–366 I provide a list of books that can serve as expert models. Feel free to use any book in your home library that has a fantastical setting.

Also note that students will need a copy of *The Hobbit* for an activity in Module 16.

The Writing Process

I use this assignment to unpack the writing process shown on xxiv–xxv in the Student Text and Workbook. As with the six traits of good writing, experienced writers will move through this process in a more holistic way—composing, revising, getting feedback, and editing as they go. I realize that walking through these steps in a systematic, linear fashion may be frustrating for some writers who already do many of these steps simultaneously or young writers who think that a first draft is the final draft. Use your best persuasive skills to convince your kids to just embrace the process in this unit. At the least, it will help you identify the steps students are not taking enough time with or do not fully understand.

13.4 Know Your Readers

Inexperienced writers typically do not understand their audiences. To be fair, many student writing assignments do not have an authentic audience because they are primarily designed for grading purposes. I want students to have real audiences in this series because real writers always write for an audience and that audience shapes what they say and how they say it. To give students a deeper understanding of how their audience should shape what they write, I ask them to choose a particular young listener as the intended audience for their fantastical tale.

I have had great success with this assignment in live co-op classes, so I hope you will see a lot of growth in your child's writing skills during this final unit. Typically, both the student writer and the young listener love the experience.

The Narrator and Point of View

If students have not written many short stories before, they may struggle to achieve a consistent point of view. Learning how to develop their characters, describe a fantastical setting, and construct a plot that wraps up in a decent amount of time will be challenging enough. Students who have completed *Writers in Residence*, volume 1, and other creative writing assignments should be ready for this next level of challenge.

The key point I would like students to grasp here is that the narrator of a story affects every single sentence. The narrator tells the story from his or her perspective, and that influences what information is revealed and how it is interpreted. Understanding what terms like *perspective* or *angle* mean may require further discussion and explanation on your part. I give examples in this unit, but students may do better with recent examples from their own lives to really understand how the person who tells the story filters everything through his or her point of view. As students begin to draft their stories from a particular point of view, it will be helpful to have them assume the role of the narrator they have chosen and read the draft aloud to you—infusing it with the narrator's personality, opinions, and distinguishing characteristics.

Unit 1

MODULE 1

1.7 Test 1: Who Said It?

Directions: What kinds of occupations, education, or experiences would help a person become an expert about different types of wildlife in your state? Discuss this with a parent, teacher, or writing coach, and write your ideas on the lines provided.

Answers will vary. Sample answers are provided.

Some occupations that would help a person become a wildlife expert are park ranger, wildlife rescue center worker, wildlife rehabilitator, ecologist, wildlife biologist, fishery technician, environmental scientist, wildlife veterinarian, zookeeper, and game warden. An expert in wildlife might have education in biology, ecology, wildlife management, zoology, or botany. A person might have experiences such as volunteering at a wildlife rescue center or a state park, bird watching, or working as a trail guide.

MODULE 3

3.5 When and Where to Cite

Directions: Write "yes" or "no" in the column on the right to indicate whether the information must be acknowledged or not.

To Cite or Not to Cite, That Is the Question	
Information	**Yes or No**
the average height, weight, and lifespan of your animal in sentences you write in your own words	no
a story about rehabilitating an injured animal you find online, rewritten in your own words	yes
suggestions for viewing your animal in the wild from your interviewee	yes
quotes about your animal's habits from one of your library books	yes

To Cite or Not to Cite, That Is the Question	
Information	**Yes or No**
a picture of your animal you find on the Internet that you copy and paste into your report	yes
popular methods for reducing disease and overpopulation problems that several of your reliable sources mention	no

3.7 Conventions: Titles

Directions: Use the guidelines in this section and the examples from the infographic on pages 80–81 to help you properly capitalize and format the list of titles below. Underline words that should be italicized. If you are not sure what part of speech a word is, use a dictionary to help you.

1. The Merchant of Venice (play)
2. The Lion, the Witch and the Wardrobe (book)
3. "The Coyote Is a Misunderstood Animal" (newspaper article)
4. "Top Three Signs That Birds Are Nesting near You" (web page)
5. All About Birds (website)
6. "Where the Sidewalk Ends" (poem)
7. Where the Sidewalk Ends (book of poetry)
8. Clubhouse (magazine)
9. The Incredibles (movie)

MODULE 4

4.12 Word Sleuth

Directions: Use a thesaurus to find several synonyms for each of the words in the chart on the next page. Choose words that are new to you and list them on the chart.

Answers will vary. Sample answers are provided.

Word Sleuth Synonyms	
Word	**Synonyms**
problem (n.)	conundrum, predicament, hitch, misfortune, mishap, quandary
friend (n.)	confidante, ally, associate, crony, compadre, sidekick
field (n.)	meadow, pasture, paddock, grassland
happiness (n.)	merriment, gaiety, joviality, jollity, glee, exuberance, exhilaration, rapture, jubilation
break (v.)	shatter, fracture, splinter, fragment, perforate
laugh (v.)	chortle, guffaw, titter, snicker, yuk, cackle, twitter
cut (v.)	gash, slash, lacerate, sever, graze, nick, incise, score
bright (adj.)	scintillating, luminous, radiant, lustrous, vibrant
wet (adj.)	moist, saturated, soggy, waterlogged
blue (adj.)	azure, cobalt, sapphire, indigo, aquamarine, cyan

Unit 1 Review

Directions: You may write your answers to the questions below in the space provided, or you can talk about these questions with a parent, teacher, or writing coach. You can also look over all the information in the modules you have completed to help you decide on your answers. Use the unit review to help you master the writing tips and tricks you learned about in these modules.

Some answers will vary. Sample answers are provided.

1. Name some of the sources you can use to collect information. (3 points)

To collect information, I can use the Internet, the public library, and experts.

2. In your own words, describe a systematic process for choosing a research topic. (5 points)

Identify as many topics as possible that will fit the assignment. Study the requirements for the assignment. Make sure my options live within the state and are wildlife (not pets or livestock). Think about whether I will be able to take field trips to learn more about the animals I am considering. Think about where I can find illustrations of the animals and whether I can reproduce them or if I must create my own. Use the Internet to research the different species of wildlife that live in my state. Jot down possibilities as I uncover them. Narrow the list of possibilities by choosing which class of wildlife I want to research (mammals, amphibians, fish, etc). Then generate a list of all my state's wildlife in the category I choose. Confirm the list using two or more reliable Internet sources. Identify the field trip opportunities nearby. List the three animals that interest me most. Use the library's catalog system to find nonfiction resources for each animal on my list. Record the best items available about each animal. Consider the quality of my resources, my interest in those resources, my interest in each animal, the availability of other resources, and which field trip(s) interest me most. With these things in mind, I can choose an animal for the research project.

3. Describe the two-test process you should follow to make sure the information you collect on the Internet is accurate. (3 points)

   I should gather information from reliable sources and verify the information using several sources. First, I should evaluate reliability by making sure that the person or organization providing the information is trustworthy and qualified. I should make sure that the publisher of any website used is clearly identified and that the person or organization has qualifying training or work experience. I should also make sure that the purpose of the website is clearly stated and that others who are trustworthy and qualified recommend the website as reliable. Second, I should verify the information by comparing several sources and seeing if the information appears in multiple reliable sources.

4. List the steps you should follow to safely search the Internet. (3 points)

   Always ask a parent, teacher, or writing coach for help. Choose keywords carefully. Enter keywords into the search engine. Have a parent, teacher, or writing coach help me identify that each site is safe before opening any links.

5. Name some of the ways you can find the information you need at a library. (3 points)

   Make an appointment with a staff member ahead of time. Use the library's catalog system to find a list of nonfiction resources and ask a parent or the librarian for help in understanding the information provided. Print out a list or write down the call numbers of the most promising options, locate the items on my list, and put a check mark beside the ones that I think will be helpful. If any of the items I want to review are checked out, I can ask a librarian to put them on hold to be checked out later.

6. Discuss some of the important reading strategies you should use when you are reading to learn. (5 points)

   Organize my physical space by choosing sources and deciding what order I will read them in. Decide where I will store my notes and put note-taking supplies in the study area. Make sure there is enough light.

While reading, make a list of the important topics related to my subject. Ideas for this list can be found in the table of contents for each book and on websites related to the subject. As I learn more, change my list of topics to include all of the information I want to be a part of my report. Organize smaller topics under larger topics. Use the list to help decide what to read and what to skip because I won't have time to read everything on my topic.

Make notes by connecting what I read with what I already know and what I plan to do with the information. Decide how to record notes and what kinds of information I want to include. Include both basic facts and interesting details. Jot down facts under the topics I chose in the previous step. Draw pictures if it helps me remember the information I am learning. Use sticky notes or index cards to mark important information I find in the books I am using.

Verify my information by making sure it appears in more than one reliable source. Keep track of verified information using check marks or highlighting. Assess whether information found in only one place is reliable.

When I encounter a new word, first take a guess on its meaning based on context. Then look up the definition in the dictionary.

Spread out my research over several days, making sure I rest in between sessions. Review what I have learned before reading new material.

Talk about what I am learning with friends and family. Discuss my findings with both younger and older people.

7. Explain plagiarism. What is not plagiarism? What are some things you can do to avoid plagiarizing? (5 points)

Plagiarism occurs when writers do not properly acknowledge the ideas and words of others or when they give the impression that others' words or ideas are their own. Plagiarism is not failing to acknowledge facts and common knowledge in the body of a paper. To avoid plagiarizing, I can rewrite what I learn in my own words. If I use facts or common knowledge, I should include the source in which I found them in the bibliography. If I use another writer's unique ideas or words, I should cite the source within the text and in the bibliography. When using another writer's exact words, I should always use quotation marks.

8. What kind of information should be included in a bibliography? (4 points)

A bibliography should include all the resources used to write a report, including those cited in the paper. Each entry should include all of the information someone would need to find each resource. This includes the author, the title of the source, the title of the container (such as a newspaper, magazine, TV network, or website), the publisher, the publication date, and the location (page numbers or web address).

9. Describe three ways you can incorporate the words and ideas of others in your research writing. (3 points)

First, I can use a direct quotation when the quote is interesting, shows an expert verifying my information, or uses phrasing that is unique. Second, I can also paraphrase (restate information in my own words). When paraphrasing, I can simplify or explain ideas at the same time. I can also paraphrase more than one source at a time. Third, I can incorporate the words and ideas of others by summarizing (condensing the content to only the main points).

10. How can you avoid plagiarizing the images you use in your science report? (3 points)

To avoid plagiarizing images, I must credit the source of each one. I can do this by placing the name of the organization or creator in parentheses below the image. If I do this, I don't need to include an entry for the illustration in the bibliography. However, if the image contains print information like a map or chart, I should include an entry for it in the bibliography. I must be sure to use images that are copyright free. If an image is not copyright free, I can e-mail the publisher of the book or the owner of the website in which it appears, explain my purpose for using the image, and ask for permission. If I do not receive a response to my request, I may still use the image as long as I properly credit the source and do not publish my report or offer it for any commercial purpose. This is true even for images that are protected by copyright. I must remove the image if and when the copyright owner asks me not to use it.

11. Writers collect more information than they can include in a final report. How can you decide what to include? (3 points)

I can think about what my readers will want to read. I will include information that I find interesting because that information will probably be interesting to my readers as well. I will also include details that show the connections I have made and unique things I learned in the process of researching the animal. Doing this provides readers with information they will not read anywhere else. I will also make sure that it is complete and that I haven't skipped any important topics.

Unit 2

MODULE 5

5.6 Generate Your Questions

Directions: To create a survey for your travel partners, first think about all the decisions involved in choosing a dream vacation: where to stay, what to do, how far to travel, and so on. These should be the basis of the questions you ask on your survey. Some of the categories to survey your travel companions about are listed for you on the chart provided. Add categories of your own to the Categories for Dream Vacation chart on the next page.

Answers will vary. Sample answers are provided.

Categories for Dream Vacation			
transportation	*food*	who else will go	scenery
activities	distance from home	pet policies	new adventure or old favorite
cost	accommodations	length of stay	climate

5.13 Word Sleuth

Directions: How many new words about travel can you add to your vocabulary? On the lines below, write synonyms for the words listed. You may use a thesaurus to help you.

Answers will vary. Sample answers are provided.

1. travel (n.) – expedition, excursion, journey, sightseeing, trip, trek
2. travel (v.) – journey, gallivant, tour, explore, wander, voyage
3. trip (n.) – outing, jaunt, vacation, expedition, journey, voyage, cruise
4. suitcase (n.) – valise, portmanteau, garment bag, backpack, duffel bag, satchel
5. ticket (n.) – pass, permit, token, coupon, voucher, transfer, admission, certificate

6. vacation (n.) – break, holiday, recess, respite, sabbatical, leave, furlough
7. relax (v.) – calm, unwind, recline, de-stress, rest, laze, repose
8. pleasant (adj.) – delightful, charming, agreeable, cheerful, fun, enjoyable, refreshing, satisfying, entertaining
9. exciting (adj.) – thrilling, exhilarating, stirring, gripping, invigorating, electrifying, astonishing
10. adventure (n.) – feat, exploit, experience, undertaking, thrill, excitement

MODULE 6

6.4 An Essay Burger

Directions: Study the copy you made of 5.3 Expert Model. Notice that the expert model contains five body paragraphs. Why do you think five were necessary? Write your answer to this question on the lines below.

Answers will vary. A sample answer is provided.

The author wanted to use one body paragraph to give a preview of how the essay is organized. He also used this paragraph to include the opinion of someone with firsthand experience of his proposed vacation spot. Then the author went on to address each family member, one per paragraph. He has four family members, which resulted in having five body paragraphs.

MODULE 7

7.5 Sentence Building

Directions: Using Pudge and Mad Cat or two lively characters of your own invention, write six sturdy sentences about them with the sentence parts listed. You can put your sentence parts in the order they are listed below, or you can rearrange the order. Just make sure you use all the sentence parts listed. You can even add more sentence parts if you can name the job they perform.

Answers will vary. Sample answers are provided.

1. Subject + simple predicate

   Mad Cat pounced.

2. Modifier + subject + simple predicate + modifier

   The cranky baby wailed miserably.

3. Compound subject + simple predicate (linking verb) + complement

   Mad Cat and Pudge were inseparable.

4. Subject + compound predicate + modifier (prepositional phrase)

   Pudge slurped and swallowed milk (direct object) from his bottle.

5. Connector + compound subject + simple predicate

   Suddenly, Mad Cat and Pudge disappeared.

6. Your choice: Label the sentence parts.

7.6 Review: Subject Complements

Directions: Add subjects and complements to complete the following sentences. Create subject complements that contain a noun that renames (predicate nominative) or an adjective that describes (predicate adjective) as indicated below the lines.

Answers will vary. Sample answers are provided.

1. During the winter months, trees (subject) became bare (predicate adjective).

2. Lucy (subject) and Daisy (subject) were friends (predicate nominative).

3. Apples (subject) are delicious (predicate adjective) once they are ripe.

4. Abraham Lincoln (subject) became president (predicate nominative) after the votes were counted.

5. The boys (subject) grew wiser (predicate adjective) with every passing day.

7.7 Verb Complements: Direct Objects

Directions: Complete the following sentences with verb complements. Mark the direct objects in each verb complement with the abbreviation "D.O."

Note: Answers like "She loves to dance" or "She loves to watch musicals" are perfectly acceptable. The infinitive form of the verb ("to ______") is a noun phrase, which can function as a direct object in a sentence. Infinitives will be taught in later volumes.

1. The linebacker tackled the running back (D.O.).

2. The tennis ball hit the wall (D.O.).

3. I admire Mother Teresa (D.O.).

4. She loves pancakes (D.O.).

5. The coach told a joke (D.O.).

7.8 Verb Complements: Indirect Objects

Directions: In the following sentences, label a direct object "D.O." and label an indirect object "I.O." Underline the complete verb complement. Not all of the sentences contain verb complements.

1. My brother passed me (I.O.) a piece (D.O.) of cake.

2. The policeman gave my mom (I.O.) a speeding ticket (D.O.).

3. Yesterday I gave my paper (D.O.) to my teacher.

4. The last train has left the station (D.O.).

5. He is captain of the soccer team.

   This sentence does not have a direct or an indirect object. *Captain* is a predicate nominative, and *of the soccer team* is a modifier. The verb *is* is a linking verb.

7.9 You Can Do This!

Directions: Now you try. Complete the following sentences with the missing sentence parts. You may use words or phrases to do the job required.

1. The ______soldier______ (subject) battled ______his enemy______ (verb complement) until neither could lift his sword again.

2. The princess scolded ______the jester______ (verb complement) in front of the court.

3. In the morning, the girl next door (subject) sings and whistles loudly (intransitive verb + modifier).

4. Rockefeller Center looks enormous (linking verb + subject complement).

5. The delivery (modifier) truck brought the books and toys (transitive verb + verb complement + verb complement) quickly.

Directions: Study the chart of sentence parts below. Then use the abbreviations for the job descriptions to label the underlined word or phrase in the following sentences. The first one has been done for you.

Subject (S)	Simple Predicate (P)	Connectors (X)	Modifiers (M)	Complements (C)
nouns	action verbs	conjunctives	adjectives	**Subject Complements** predicate nominatives predicate adjectives
pronouns	linking verbs	adverbs	adverbs	**Verb Complements**
		phrases	prepositional phrases	direct objects indirect objects

1. Mad Cat (S) and (X) Pudge (S) built (P) a fort (C) in the woods (M) behind the house (M).

2. The puppy (S) happily (M) brought (P) the bone (C) to his master (M).

3. My mother (S) likes (P) cereal (C) in the morning (M).

4. Mad Cat (S) was (P) hungry (C). She (S) wanted (P) blackbird pie (C).

5. Last night (M) we (S) went (P) to the opera (M).

7.10 Mastery Test

Directions: Create sentences that follow the sentence patterns specified.

Answers will vary. Sample answers are provided.

1. Compound subject + linking verb + subject complement (predicate nominative) + modifier

   Example: Sandy and Billy became cocaptains of the soccer team.

   Example: My cucumbers and tomatoes were prize winners this year.

   Tom and Jerry were enemies for many years.

2. Subject + intransitive verb + modifier

   Example: The rocket ship launched successfully.

   Example: Their house flooded during the hurricane.

   The smoke vanished without a trace.

3. Modifier + subject + transitive verb + verb complement (indirect object) + modifier + verb complement (direct object)

   Example: The beautiful girl handed the prince her glass slipper.

   Example: The relief pitcher threw the batter a curve ball.

   The patient mother gave her mischievous son a kiss.

4. Subject + compound predicate + modifier

Example: The firewood crackled and burned brightly.

Example: The crows squawked and cawed angrily.

The waves crashed and receded rhythmically.

5. Subject + transitive verb + verb complement (direct object)

Example: The ball hit the rim.

Example: The car ran a red light.

The lion chased the antelope.

MODULE 8

8.3 Voice: A Writer's Fingerprints

Directions: On the lines provided, describe the kind of personality you think the writer of the expert model has. List some of the clues in his essay that help you to decide.

Answers will vary. A sample answer is provided.

I think the writer is enthusiastic. I know this because he uses words like "perfect," "thrilling," and "best vacation ever." He also uses exclamation points, which make it seem like he is speaking loudly and excitedly.

He is observant too. He remembers what Grammy has said ("If you're happy, I'm happy"). He knows the kinds of shops his mom and grandmother would enjoy exploring. He knows that his mother likes to work out in the morning and that long car rides are exhausting to his dad. It is clear that he pays attention to his family members.

I think he is also funny. He starts with "Attention, family!" as if he is making an official announcement. He teases his dad for being his "worst critic." And he says, "I'm taking no chances of that happening!" about the idea of having to rewrite his essay over and over. He seems like someone who enjoys humor, and this shows in his writing.

8.8 Inspect and Improve: Sentence Structure

Directions: Answer the questions about the sentences below. Sentence parts we have not studied yet appear in gray.

1. We have won a dream vacation to the destination of our choice.

What is the subject? "We" is the subject.

What is the simple predicate? "Have won" is the simple predicate.

What job is *a dream vacation* performing in this sentence?

"Dream vacation" is a verb complement.

To the destination and *of our choice* are both performing the same job.

What is it? They are both modifiers.

2. The It's-A-Doozy Travel Company awarded us five hundred dollars each for our trip.

What is the complete subject? The complete subject is "The It's-A-Doozy Travel Company."

What is the simple predicate? The simple predicate is "awarded."

What grammatical unit is *five hundred dollars*? "Five hundred dollars" is a verb complement. It includes a direct object, "dollars."

What sentence part is *us*? "Us" is an indirect object.

3. The nearby town boasts many used bookstores and antique stores for you and Mom to explore.

What kind of verb is *boasts* in this sentence? "Boasts" is used as a transitive verb in this sentence.

What is the complete subject? The complete subject is "the nearby town."

What two sentence parts are compound? There is a compound direct object ("bookstores and stores") and a compound object of a preposition ("you and Mom").

What is the complete verb complement of this sentence? The complete verb complement is "many used bookstores and antique stores for you and Mom to explore."

4. Or you can enjoy a leisurely stroll along the beach and take a dip when you get hot.

What words function as connectors in this sentence? The words "or" and "and" are connectors.

What is the subject of this sentence? The subject of the sentence is "you."

The verbs *enjoy* and *take* form what kind of predicate? They form a compound simple predicate.

What sentence part is *a dip*? "Dip" is a direct object.

Unit 2 Review

Directions: You may write your answers to the questions below and on the next two pages in the space provided, or you can talk about these questions with a parent, teacher, or writing coach. You can also look over all the information in the modules you have completed to help you decide on your answers. Use the unit review to help you master the writing tips and tricks you learned about in these modules.

1. What are some of the sources writers use to form an opinion based on solid evidence? (3 points)

They gather and analyze data using surveys. They also interview experts and people with firsthand experience. Writers also use verified facts that they gather from the Internet or printed sources.

2. What are all the parts of an essay burger? What should be included in the introduction and body paragraphs? (10 points)

The parts of the essay burger are the introduction, the body paragraphs, and the conclusion. The introduction should include a hook, some background information, and the thesis. Each body paragraph should have its own logical reason supported by facts, apt examples, and details. The conclusion should seal the deal and close the circle. One way to do this is to hint at something in the introduction and then reveal it in the conclusion.

3. What are some of the ways writers support their logical reasons? (4 points)

Writers support their logical reasons with carefully researched facts that answer who, what, when, where, why, and how about their reasons. They also use specific examples, and they can support their reasons with details that add even more information.

4. What is a thesis? Where should it appear? (2 points)

A thesis is a position to be discussed or proven through a written or oral argument. It should appear in the introductory paragraph. Readers expect to find it there, and it lets them know the purpose of the essay right away. If the thesis isn't in the introduction, readers do not understand the reason for the evidence presented in the rest of the essay.

5. Describe each of the six traits of good writing in your own words. (6 points)

Answers will vary. A sample answer is provided.

Ideas: It is important to have a clear idea of what I am setting out to prove and to support my ideas with logical reasons and solid evidence.

Organization: My writing should follow a structure that makes sense. In essay writing, this means that my piece will have an introduction, body paragraphs, and a conclusion and that all of the sentences in each section will serve the purpose of that particular section.

Voice: My writing should sound like me. I can accomplish this by using a specific tone, showing my emotions through punctuation and wording, or including humor. My voice should stay consistent throughout the piece.

Sentence structure: It is important to build my sentences carefully so that each sentence part is doing the job it needs to do. This will make my writing understandable and enjoyable to read.

Word choice: I should be sure to use nouns, verbs, and modifiers that are interesting and do a good job of showing exactly what I'm trying to say. It's also important not to repeat words but to find new ways of saying things.

Conventions: I need to follow the rules of capitalization, punctuation, spelling, and usage. This is so that readers can follow what I am saying and not be distracted by mistakes.

6. What are some of the strategies for injecting voice into your writing that you have learned so far in the *Writers in Residence* series? (5 points)

Answers will vary. A sample answer is provided.

In an essay, I can use a specific tone (attitude), certain punctuation marks, carefully chosen words, and humor to inject my voice.

7. What is an important consideration when deciding how to organize the information in an essay? (1 point)

An important thing to consider is how to make it easy for readers to follow my logic.

8. What is the purpose of transitional words and phrases in an argument essay? (2 points)

Transitional words and phrases show connections between ideas and indicate what is coming next. In this way, they make an argument easier for readers to follow.

9. What are two things you should try to do in the conclusion of an argument essay? (2 points)

I should try to seal the deal (win the approval of the readers) and close the circle (make a link between the introduction and the conclusion).

10. Name the five jobs sentence parts can perform in a sentence. (5 points)

Sentence parts can be subjects, simple predicates, modifiers, connectors, or complements.

Unit 3

MODULE 9

9.3 What Makes a Poem a Poem?

Directions: On the lines below, describe some of the things you noticed about poetry from studying these poems. What characteristics help you recognize that these are poems and not prose?

Answers will vary. A sample answer is provided.

The shape of a poem is not like prose writing, where the sentences go from line to line, separated by punctuation and capital letters. There seems to be more freedom in the writing of poetry when it comes to rules of capitalization and punctuation. Poems sound different from prose when they are read aloud. Poems have a pattern of syllables or sound that repeats. Some of them rhyme. Some of them include metaphors that paint a picture in the reader's mind. Some of them repeat vowel or consonant sounds.

9.7 The Sound of Music

Directions: How many words can you think of that rhyme with the words below? Write them on the chart.

Answers will vary. Sample answers are provided.

Rhyme It				
shirt	**elbow**	**forget**	**grew**	**choir**
skirt	*echo*	*regret*	*knew*	*wire*
dirt hurt Bert	blow crow row	let bet wet	flew dew cue	liar fire brier

Continued on next page »

Rhyme It				
shirt	**elbow**	**forget**	**grew**	**choir**
pert squirt assert subvert yurt convert blurt spurt dessert	willow show sew ago banjo glow know dough meadow	barrette duet clarinet pet threat debt vet outlet sunset	construe new blue woo statue subdue cashew glue shampoo	shire flier prior buyer higher conspire umpire tire fryer

Directions: Write an alliterative sentence for each of the words listed below.

Answers will vary. Sample answers are provided.

Alliterate	
kite	*The king's kite, cut loose by the count, climbed above the clouds, careening and cartwheeling as it went.*
peppermint	Peter was pleased to passionately partake of the peppermint pie.
mud	Munching marshmallows, the mischievous mouse marched through the mud to the mansion for more treats.
rodeo	The redheaded cowboy returned to the rodeo with rare reluctance, no longer raring to risk his life.
bake	Beverly's beautiful boss will bake a Boston cream pie before breakfast.

Directions: On the chart below, list words that repeat the final consonant sound of each word on the chart without repeating the vowel sound.

Answers will vary. Sample answers are provided.

Create Consonance			
pit	**garden**	**call**	**splash**
spot	began	hail	fresh
bat	train	bell	squish
ferret	stun	treadmill	swordfish
shout	explain	seagull	wash
what	green	pal	thrush
treat	shine	squeal	quiche
late	alone	mile	dish
night	moon	troll	gauche
feet	coin	tadpole	swoosh
flute	lawn	jewel	unleash

Directions: Write sentences that repeat the following vowel sounds. Remember that the spelling of the words can vary, but the vowel sound must be the same.

Answers will vary. Sample answers are provided.

1. Long ū as in *cube*. True friends are few, but they are proven when you are blue.
2. Short ĭ as in *slip*. Six silly pigs winked as they spilled the glistening liquid into the sink.
3. Long ē as in *bee*. Steve keeps leaving creepy green beetles in Lee's cleats.

9.8 Expert Model

Directions: Answer the questions about the sound devices in "A Boat Beneath a Sunny Sky."

Answers will vary. Sample answers are provided.

1. What sound device does Carroll use in the title and opening line of the poem?

   Carroll uses alliteration in the title and opening line by repeating the "b" sound.

2. Find an example of assonance in the poem.

   There is assonance in the third stanza:

   "Long has paled that sunny sky:
   Echoes fade and memories die:
   Autumn frosts have slain July."

   The long "a" sound is repeated ("paled," "fade," "slain"), the short "o" sound is repeated ("long," "Autumn," "frosts), and the long "i" sound is repeated ("sky," "die," "July").

3. With what other lines does the word *phantomwise* in line 10 rhyme?

   "Phantomwise" rhymes with line 11 ("skies") and line 12 ("eyes").

4. List some of the words repeated in the poem.

   The following words are repeated: "dream/dreaming," "eye/eyes," "sky/skies," "ear," "near," and "hear."

5. Find an example of consonance in the poem.

   The "ing" sound is a repeated consonant sound throughout the poem. For example, in stanza 1 see "lingering" and "evening." In stanza 4 see "moving" and "waking."

MODULE 10

10.3 The Rhythm of Poetry

Directions: Try it and see: Put your hand under your chin and say the following words. Decide which part of the word is stressed. Underline it.

Roger

concoction

blanket

happy

democracy

decide

begin

revelation

Directions: Try to identify the stressed syllable by saying the following words aloud. Underline the stressed syllable of each word. Then check your guess with a dictionary.

1. sun ny

2. un sui ta ble

3. gal lop ing

4. al mond

5. am bi tious

6. bul let

7. de li cious

8. writ er

9. per for mance

10. ac tiv i ty

10.5 Repetition—A Poet's Friend

Directions: Fill out the chart with some of the repeated words and phrases you notice in the following poems.

Repeated Words and Phrases			
"Be Glad Your Nose Is on Your Face" (page 239)	**"The Railway Train" (page 240)**	**"Seal" (page 245)**	**"A Boat Beneath a Sunny Sky" (page 250)**
your nose if	and then	"see how he" "before you can" and	"dream/ dreaming" "eye/eyes" "sky/skies" ear near hear "dreaming as"

10.8 Cinquain Train

Directions: Answer the following questions about the cinquains by Adelaide Crapsey.

Answers will vary. Sample answers are provided.

1. What does the title "Niagara" refer to?

   The title refers to Niagara Falls.

2. In your own words, describe the image the poem "Niagara" is based on.

   The poem describes a pale moon in the sky above a huge, crashing waterfall.

3. What is the home referred to in the poem "The Grand Canyon"? Whom is it for?

   The home referred to is the Grand Canyon. The writer believes it would be suitable for giants, gods, and heroes.

4. Why does Adelaide Crapsey think this is a fitting home for those named in the poem?
   She thinks it is a fitting home because it is so huge and awe-inspiring.

5. In "November Night," what sounds "like steps of passing ghosts"?
   Falling leaves sound like steps of passing ghosts.

MODULE 11 WRITER'S WORKSHOP

11.2 Review Your Progress

Directions: Fill in the blanks to make the sentences complete and accurate.

1. Complements follow the verb and complete the sentence. __Transitive__ verbs and __linking__ verbs require complements. __Intransitive__ verbs do not.

2. __Subject__ complements follow a(n) __linking__ verb. They rename or describe the subject of the sentence. If the subject complement renames the subject, it is a predicate __nominative__. If the subject complement describes the subject, then it is a predicate __adjective__.

3. __Verb__ complements follow a(n) __transitive__ verb. They complete the action of the verb. A(n) __direct__ object is a verb complement that answers the question *Whom?* or *What?* A(n) __indirect__ object is a verb complement that answers the question *To whom?* or *For whom?*

4. A(n) __indirect__ object never appears without a(n) __direct__ object, and it always comes before the __direct__ object.

Directions: Answer the questions about the following lines of poetry.

Answers will vary. Sample answers are provided.

"The fog comes / on little cat feet." ("Fog" by Carl Sandburg)

1. What is the subject of this sentence?

   The subject is "fog."

2. What is the simple predicate of this sentence?

   The simple predicate is "comes."

3. What type of phrase is *on little cat feet*?

   "On little cat feet" is a prepositional phrase.

4. What job is *on little cat feet* doing in this sentence?

   "On little cat feet" modifies the predicate (telling how the fog came).

"Autumn frosts have slain July." ("A Boat Beneath a Sunny Sky" by Lewis Carroll)

1. What job is *Autumn* doing in this sentence?

   In this sentence, "Autumn" is an adjective that modifies "frosts."

2. What part of speech is *frosts*?

   "Frosts" is a noun.

3. What kind of complement is *July*?

   "July" is a direct object.

4. What type of verb does the complement *July* make *have slain*?

   The complement "July" makes "have slain" a transitive verb.

"Swift things are beautiful." ("Swift Things Are Beautiful" by Elizabeth Coatsworth)

1. What is the subject of this line of poetry?

   The subject of this line is "things."

2. What type of verb appears in this line of poetry?

   There is a linking verb ("are") in this line.

3. What specific type of complement is *beautiful*? Explain how you decided.

   "Beautiful" is a predicate adjective. I know this because it follows a linking verb and describes the subject.

"He took his vorpal sword in hand." ("Jabberwocky" by Lewis Carroll)

1. What part of speech is the made-up word *vorpal*?

   "Vorpal" is an adjective.

2. What job is *in hand* performing?

   "In hand" is doing the job of a modifier.

3. What is the complement in this sentence? What type of object is in it?

   The complement is "his vorpal sword." "Sword" is a direct object because it answers the question "What did he take in his hand?"

11.5 Antecedents

Directions: In the following sentences, underline each pronoun that is used with an antecedent. Draw an arrow from the pronoun to its antecedent.

Answers will vary. Sample answers are provided.

1. Mrs. Wilson said <u>she</u> planned to sign up for the field trip online.

2. The book is perfect for toddlers. <u>It</u> includes a lot of funny pictures and very few words.

3. When Liam had enough money, he bought a better catcher's mitt.

4. By the time my family arrived at the game, they were already fifteen minutes late.

5. Every time I race my sister, she comes closer to beating me.

6. That was the best movie I have seen in a long time.

7. I told the librarian these were the books I wanted to check out.

8. Mandy and Sam told the officer the lost dog was theirs.

11.6 Personal Pronouns

Directions: Complete the following sentences by placing a personal pronoun in each blank to make the sentences grammatically correct. Remember to use a pronoun from the subject columns to replace a subject or subject complement. Use a pronoun from the object columns if the sentence part must be a direct object, indirect object, or object of a preposition.

Answers will vary. Sample answers are provided.

1. ___We___ are going to the library on Wednesday. Would ___you___ like to go with ___us___?

2. Jack forgot to bring something to write on. Miranda had an extra notebook with ___her___, so ___she___ offered ___it___ to ___him___.

3. Miranda told ___me___ that ___we___ should meet ___her___ at the library. ___She___ said to bring ___her___ a snack.

4. ___I___ don't understand this problem. Can ___you___ show ___me___ how to solve ___it___?

5. The packages are scheduled to arrive tomorrow. Where should ___he___ put ___them___ when ___they___ arrive?

6. Raymond is expecting a letter. Is this for ___him___?

11.7 Possessive Pronoun or Possessive Adjective?

Directions: Look at these examples. Decide if the italicized word is a pronoun or an adjective. Determine what job the word is doing to help you decide. Write "Pro." above the pronouns and "Adj." above the adjectives.

1. This book is *his*. (Pro.)
2. This is *his* book. (Adj.)
3. Jane left *her* (Adj.) sweater in the back of the van. *This* (Adj.) one must be *hers*. (Pro.)
4. *Their* (Adj.) house is on the left.
5. The brick house is *theirs*. (Pro.)
6. I put *my* (Adj.) leftovers in the refrigerator. This has to be *mine*. (Pro.)
7. We are going to *your* (Adj.) game tonight.
8. This mess is *yours* (Pro.), not *mine* (Pro.).

11.11 Word Sleuth

Directions: Use a dictionary and a box of crayons to help you complete this assignment. Fill in the chart below with new color words and their definitions. You may find that an unfamiliar word on your crayon is not listed in your dictionary as a color but as something that inspired the color. (For example, a manatee is a gray marine animal, and goldenrod is a perennial herb with yellow flowers.) That's okay. Write whatever definition you find. The purpose of this exercise is to learn some new words.

Answers will vary. Sample answers are provided.

Precise Color Words	
Color Word	**Definition**
russet	reddish brown
aquamarine	pale blue to light greenish blue
periwinkle	light purplish blue
indigo	deep reddish blue
fuchsia	vivid reddish purple
cerise	moderate red
cerulean	resembling the blue of sky

MODULE 12

12.3 The Inventiveness of Poetry

Directions: Look at the lines from "A Boat Beneath a Sunny Sky" on the next page. Now that you know poets can omit words, rearrange their order, and use them in new ways, can you figure out the answers to the questions that correspond with each line? Some of the questions may seem difficult; just do your best. The number of the question corresponds with the same numbered line of the poem.

(1) Long has paled that sunny sky:

(2) Echoes fade and memories die:

(3) Autumn frosts have slain July.

(4) Still she haunts me, phantomwise,

(5) Alice moving under skies

(6) Never seen by waking eyes.

Answers will vary. Sample answers are provided.

1. Write a complete sentence that explains what "Long has paled that sunny sky" means.

It has been a long time since the sunny day that the writer is remembering.

2. This line leaves questions unanswered. What echoes do you think have faded? What memories do you think have died?

The echoes of the children talking and the writer telling his tales have faded. Memories of all the details of the day in July have faded (for the writer and for the children as well).

3. What do you think this line means? What aspects of July have been slain?

I think the line means that the changing of seasons (the passing of time) has done away with the pleasant days that the writer is remembering. The frosts have slain July's carefree, dreamy feeling and the clear memories of that time. There is also a sense that the children's youth is slain by the passing of time.

4. What does the poet mean when he says Alice "haunts" him? Is she dead?

She is not necessarily dead. The poet means that the memory of Alice returns to him like a ghost. He does not see her in real life anymore, but experiencing his memory of her is like being visited by a phantom.

5. Why is Alice moving?

Alice is moving because she is floating in a boat and the boat is moving.

6. What is never seen by waking eyes?

The skies are never seen by waking eyes. In this stanza, the skies are part of the poet's remembrance or a dream world that he has created, so they are not actually seen by the children.

12.4 Denotations and Connotations of Words

Directions: Fill in the chart with synonyms with both positive and negative connotations that are similar in denotative meaning to each word listed. The first one has been done for you.

Answers will vary. Sample answers are provided.

Positive and Negative Connotations		
Word	**Positive Synonym**	**Negative Synonym**
small	petite	puny
stubborn	persistent	obstinate
talkative	sociable	long-winded
excited	enthusiastic	nervous
young	youthful	immature

12.5 Metaphor and Simile

Directions: Answer these questions about the two poems you just read.

Answers will vary. Sample answers are provided.

1. To what does Carl Sandburg compare the fog? Which words in the poem help you to recognize the metaphor?

   Carl Sandburg compares the fog to a cat. I recognize the metaphor from the words "little cat feet" and "silent haunches."

2. How are these two things alike?

   They are alike in that they are both quiet. They don't make a scene; they are just present and then gone.

3. Create your own metaphor. What object, idea, or experience would you compare the fog with?

   The fog is a blindfold, forcing me to carefully feel my way along.

4. To what does Amy Sklansky compare the moon?

   Amy Sklansky compares the moon to a night-light.

5. How are these two things alike?

   They both glow at night. They both provide a sense of comfort.

6. To what object, idea, or experience would you compare the moon?

   I would compare the moon to a lighthouse guiding ships on the ocean.

Directions: Find two similes and one metaphor in the poem on the next page. Write them on the lines below. Then describe the two things being compared in each example. This poem does not have a title. Choose one for it and write it on the line above the poem.

Answers will vary. Sample answers are provided.

"Like magic" and "clear as glass" are similes. "Thin green sticks" is a metaphor. In the first example, the poet is comparing the dragonfly rising from the weeds to magic. In the second, she is comparing the dragonfly's wings to glass. In the third, she is comparing the insect's body and wings to sticks.

Sample title: "The Magical Dragonfly"

12.6 Allusion Infusion

Directions: Answer the questions about the allusions in the following sentences.

The football game this weekend will be another David versus Goliath.

1. "David versus Goliath" is an allusion to what work of art, literature, or historical event?

"David versus Goliath" is an allusion to the account in 1 Samuel of the boy David defeating the giant Goliath with a stone and a sling.

2. Describe what the allusion suggests will happen at the football game.

The allusion suggests that the teams will be unfairly matched, with one team having players who are much larger or more skilled than those of the other team. However, the allusion also suggests that the underdogs will win.

Put your John Hancock right here.

1. Who was "John Hancock"?

John Hancock was a leader in the American Revolution and a signer of the Declaration of Independence. His signature was the largest one on the document.

2. What does this statement instruct you to do?

It instructs you to sign something.

The twins are named Joshua and Caleb.

1. The twins' names are an allusion to whom?

The twins' names are an allusion to two of the twelve Israelite men who were chosen to spy out the Promised Land after the Israelites came out of Egypt. Joshua and Caleb were the only two spies who had enough faith in God that they were not fearful to take the land; they knew that if God told them to do it, He would help them complete the task.

2. Why do you think their parents chose these names for their sons?

Their parents probably hoped that they would grow up to be men of faith and boldness.

Amelia is a real Einstein.

1. What is the allusion in this sentence?

   The allusion is to Albert Einstein, the famous German physicist.

2. What do you think Amelia is like?

   I think she is extremely intelligent and creative.

It was a 9/11 event for the small town.

1. What does "9/11" allude to?

   The date "9/11" alludes to a series of terrorist attacks on the United States that took place on September 11, 2001.

2. What kind of event do you think occurred?

   It was a tragic, life-changing event.

Don't be a Scrooge!

1. What is the allusion?

   This sentence is an allusion to A Christmas Carol by Charles Dickens. The main character's name is Ebenezer Scrooge.

2. What do you think the person being addressed is doing?

   The person being addressed is probably being greedy and unwilling to share because this is the kind of character Ebenezer Scrooge is. Or he might be expressing dislike for Christmas celebrations.

Randall, you have a nose as long as Pinocchio's.

1. Who is Pinocchio?

   Pinocchio is the name of a character in a children's story called The Adventures of Pinocchio. He is a wooden puppet who wants to be a real boy. When he lies (which is a frequent habit), his nose grows.

2. What does this statement tell you about Randall?

   Randall is also in the habit of lying.

Directions: Read the entire poem "A Boat Beneath a Sunny Sky" on page 250 aloud again. Pay attention to the sounds, rhythm, connotations of the words, and the allusion in the final line. Then answer the following questions.

1. Why do you think Lewis Carroll concludes the poem with an allusion to "Row, Row, Row Your Boat"? How does it reinforce an emotion or idea in his poem?

   I think he concludes with this allusion because it fits the theme of his poem, which is the joy and fleeting nature of childhood. It reinforces the idea that some moments of life are dreamlike, and that sometimes we are able to relive moments only in our daydreams.

2. What emotions do you experience as you think about the poem?

   I experience a yearning to be in the scene and experience the coziness and serenity the poet describes. I also feel a little sad to think about how life's good times pass by and are gone so quickly.

3. What experiences in your own life does Carroll's poem remind you of?

   His poem reminds me of my grandfather telling me stories. It reminds me of cuddling with my mom. It also reminds me of lying on the beach in the sun and feeling sleepy.

Unit 3 Review

Directions: To show how much you have learned in this unit about poetry, carefully study the poem "The Railway Train" by Emily Dickinson. Before you begin, look up any words in the poem that you do not already know. Then answer the questions about the poem on the lines below. You may talk about your answers with a parent, teacher, or writing coach in advance.

Directions: Answer these questions about this poem by Emily Dickinson.

1. In the first line, to what or whom does the pronoun *it* refer? (2 points)

   "It" refers to a train.

2. How does Emily Dickinson create sound in the first stanza? Give examples. (3 points)

Dickinson creates sound in the first stanza by using rhyme, alliteration, and assonance.

3. To what is the railway train compared in this poem? Is this a metaphor or simile? (2 points)

The railway train is compared to a huge horse. This is a metaphor.

4. Since the comparison is not directly stated, list some of the individual words in the poem that show the comparison. (5 points)

Some of the words that show the comparison are "lick," "feed," "step," "peer," "chase," "neigh," and "stable."

5. How many syllables are in lines 1 and 3? How many stressed beats are in each of these lines? (2 points)

Lines 1 and 3 contain eight syllables each. Each line has four stressed beats.

6. How many syllables in lines 2 and 4? How many stressed beats are in each of these lines? (2 points)

Lines 2 and 4 contain six syllables each. Each line has three stressed beats.

7. List some of the nouns Emily Dickinson uses in this poem. (5 points)

Emily Dickinson uses the nouns "miles," "valleys," "tanks," "mountains," "shanties," "roads," "quarry," "sides," "hill," "Boanerges," "star," and "door."

8. List some of the verbs Emily Dickinson uses in this poem. (5 points)

Emily Dickinson uses the verbs "like," "lap," "lick," "stop," "feed," "step," "peer," "pare," "crawl," "complaining," "chase," "neigh," and "stop."

9. What sound device is *horrid, hooting*? (2 points)

This is an example of alliteration.

10. What is the allusion Emily Dickinson uses in the poem? What additional meaning is added through this allusion? *Boanerges* is an example of what figure of speech? (2 points)

"Boanerges" is an example of allusion. It means "Sons of Thunder," and it refers to James and John in the Bible. I think the additional meaning here is that the train is loud and thunderous as it travels. "Boanerges" is a simile because the word "like" comes before it in the poem.

11. How does the meter of the last two lines change? Why do you think Emily Dickinson changed it? (3 points)

The second-to-last line has a different meter than this line in the other stanzas. It makes the reader slow down. I think Emily Dickinson changed it to match the subject of the stanza. She is describing the train stopping and becoming "docile." Because the reader also must stop and pause, this helps create the mood of the poem's conclusion.

12. What figure of speech is *punctual as a star*? (2 points)

"Punctual as a star" is an example of simile.

Unit 4

MODULE 13

13.3 The Writing Process

Directions: Use the infographic "Introduction to the Writing Process" on the preceding page to answer the questions below.

Answers will vary. Sample answers are provided.

1. In step 1 the writer plans. What are some of the things you think a writer might think about before beginning to draft a fiction writing project?

   A writer might think about who the audience will be for his project. A writer might also think about what the setting and main character will be like. He might also think about what the big problem (conflict) will be.

2. Step 1 also notes that a writer discusses. With whom do you think a writer discusses a writing project?

   A student writer could discuss a writing project with a parent or teacher. He could also discuss it and brainstorm with other student writers who are tackling the same project. A writer could also discuss the idea for the project with the intended audience to learn more about what might make a story appealing.

3. In step 3 the writer reviews. What aspects of a story do you think a writer might "inspect and improve" and "get feedback from readers" about after the first draft?

   A writer might get feedback on the general idea for the story, if the characters seem believable, if the plot is interesting and moves forward at a good pace, if the conflict seems engaging, and if the details about the setting and characters help paint a vivid picture in the readers' minds.

4. During what stages of the writing process does a writer involve others? How do you think other people can help you with a writing project?

   A writer involves others during planning, reviewing, editing, polishing and publishing, and evaluating. I think other people can help me by discussing my plan with me; reviewing my drafts and giving feedback; helping me check grammar, spelling, punctuation, and capitalization; reading or hearing my final product; and helping me identify the strengths and weaknesses of my project.

5. Why do you think a student writer studies the rubric at the beginning of a writing project and again before the final draft?

   A writer studies the rubric before writing to find out what the expectations or goals of the project are. There are a lot of things to keep in mind when writing, and it is helpful to have them all in one place. Studying the rubric can help guide him as he writes. He studies it again before the final draft to make sure he has done everything on it. At this point, the rubric serves as a checklist to help make sure the final draft is as good as it can be.

6. Why is it important to share a finished writing project with some readers?

   Writers write for readers. It is impossible to know if my writing is communicating my thoughts clearly or having the impact that I hope it will if other people aren't reading it and giving me feedback.

7. Why do you think a writer evaluates the strengths and weaknesses of a piece of writing after the project is finished?

   Writing is hard work! Taking time to evaluate the strengths of a writing project helps writers remember that, despite seeing places to improve all along the way, there are many things to celebrate and savor. A writer can also learn important things to apply to her next writing project. She may even want to further revise that piece of writing to make it still stronger!

13.8 Fantastical Creatures Who Walk and Talk

Directions: On the Famous Fantastical Villains chart on the next page, list some of the famous antagonists you can recall from fantasy or fairy tales. Put a star beside the one you think is the best villain an author has created.

Answers will vary. Sample answers are provided.

Famous Fantastical Villains	
Villain	**Title**
The White Witch	*The Lion, the Witch and the Wardrobe*
Smaug	The Hobbit
Maleficent	"Sleeping Beauty"
the evil queen	"Snow White"
the wolf	"Little Red Riding Hood"
the witch	"Hansel and Gretel"
Captain Hook	Peter Pan
the Horned King	The Book of Three

MODULE 14

14.4 First-Person Point of View

Directions: Find a favorite book with a first-person point of view. If you have used *Readers in Residence*, volume 1, *Because of Winn-Dixie* or *Sarah, Plain and Tall* will work well for this assignment. Page through multiple sections of the book at different stages of the plot, and then answer the questions.

Answers will vary. Sample answers are provided.

1. Find two examples in the book where you know what the narrator is thinking or feeling. Describe what is revealed.

In *Because of Winn-Dixie*, Opal is praying to God at the end of chapter five. I learn that she prays for her Mama and that she hopes to tell her Mama the story of Winn-Dixie and the mouse one day. I learn that she is lonely in Naomi and that the kids she knows don't seem like they will be friends. I also learn that she is tenderhearted enough to pray that the mouse had a soft landing when he went flying out the door of the church.

Later on, in chapter 17, I read that Opal was about to stick out her tongue when she rode by the Dewberrys' house but that she remembered some of the words of Gloria Dump and Miss Franny and decided to wave instead.

2. Review the major events in the book. How does the narrator know what happens?

The narrator (Opal) knows what happens because she is present for all of the major events. They involve her.

3. Are there any significant events in the book where the narrator isn't a part of the action? How does the narrator find out what happens?

There is important background information about each character that Opal learns when the characters tell her their stories (or sometimes when one character tells her information about another). Also, while Opal and her father are out looking for Winn-Dixie, some important things happen at the party (like the Dewberrys learning that Gloria isn't a witch, Gloria and Franny singing for the children, and Otis finding Winn-Dixie). Opal finds out about this when she and her father return to the party and Gloria tells her about it.

14.5 Third-Person Point of View

Directions: Review 11.4–11.7 and then circle all the personal pronouns and possessive adjectives in the expert model above. Label each one first, second, or third person.

EXPERT MODEL

"Where's Papa going with that ax?" said Fern to her (third) mother as they (third) were setting the table for breakfast.

"Out to the hoghouse," replied Mrs. Arable. "Some pigs were born last night."

"I (first) don't see why he (third) needs an ax," continued Fern, who was only eight.

"Well," said her (third) mother, "one of the pigs is a runt. It's (third) very small and weak, and it (third) will never amount to anything. So your (second) father has decided to do away with it (third)."

"Do *away* with it (third)?" shrieked Fern. "You (second) mean *kill* it (third)? Just because it's (third) smaller than the others?"

Mrs. Arable put a pitcher of cream on the table. "Don't yell, Fern!" she (third) said. "Your (second) father is right. The pig would probably die anyway." (1)

Directions: Rewrite the opening of Charlotte's Web from a first-person point of view. Use Fern as the narrator. Don't forget to include some of what Fern is thinking and feeling.

Answers will vary. Sample answers are provided.

"Where's Papa going with that ax?" I asked my mother as we were setting the table for breakfast. I was surprised to see him carrying it so early in the morning. He usually didn't split wood until after lunchtime.

"Out to the hoghouse," replied Mama. "Some pigs were born last night."

"I don't see why he needs an ax," I said, hoping she would explain.

"Well," said Mama, "one of the pigs is a runt. It's very small and weak, and it will never amount to anything. So your father has decided to do away with it."

My mind was reeling. I could not believe what she was saying.

"Do *away* with it?" I shrieked. "You mean *kill* it? Just because it's smaller than the others?"

I thought of the tiny pig in the hoghouse, not even knowing that his life would soon be cruelly ended. I could not bear the thought.

Mama put a pitcher of cream on the table. "Don't yell, Fern!" she said. "Your father is right. The pig would probably die anyway."

MODULE 15 WRITER'S WORKSHOP

15.1 Review Your Progress

Directions: Fill in the blanks to make the sentences complete and accurate.

1. **Complements** follow the verb and complete the sentence.

   ______Transitive______ **verbs** and ______linking______ **verbs** require complements. ______Intransitive______ **verbs** do not.

2. ______Subject______ **complements** follow a(n) ______linking______ **verb**. They rename or describe the subject of the sentence. If the subject complement **renames** the subject, it is a **predicate** ______nominative______. If the subject complement **describes** the subject, then it is a **predicate** ______adjective______ .

3. ______Verb______ **complements** follow a(n) ______transive______ **verb.** They complete the action of the verb. A(n) ______direct______ **object** is a verb complement that answers the question *Whom?* or *What?* A(n) ______indirect______ **object** is a verb complement that answers the question *To whom?* or *For whom?*

4. A(n) ______indirect______ **object** never appears without a(n) ______direct______ **object**, and it always precedes the ______direct______ **object**.

Directions: Answer the questions about personal pronouns and possessive adjectives. Use module 11 to help you.

1. Pronouns, like conjunctions and prepositions, are function words. Explain in your own words what function words do.

   Function words show how other sentence parts are related to each other.

2. Why should writers pay special attention to the pronouns they use in their writing?

   Pronouns take the place of nouns or represent nouns that are understood. They always refer to something or someone else. It is important for writers to make sure they are using the correct pronouns to keep their readers from being confused.

3. What is an antecedent? Write a sentence that contains an antecedent.

   An antecedent is the noun or pronoun that a pronoun replaces.

   Example: The dog chased its tail.

4. A personal pronoun indicates four things about the noun it replaces. What are they?

   A personal pronoun indicates person, number, gender, and function.

5. How can you tell the difference between a possessive pronoun and a possessive adjective?

   A possessive pronoun replaces the noun (as in "that book is his"). A possessive adjective precedes a noun and modifies it (as in "his book").

6. Which element of their poems and stories do poets and storytellers use pronouns to help them establish?

   Poets and storyteller use pronouns to help establish a consistent point of view.

15.3 Why Pronouns Matter

Directions: Read the passage again and cross out the nouns that you think the author replaced with pronouns in the original paragraph. Write the pronoun or possessive adjective you believe he used above the noun.

The sun was shining, the cool of morning was losing ground to a hot summer sun, and Janner was imagining that ~~Janner~~ *he* could fly. ~~Janner~~ *He* was watching the dragonflies float across the pasture, putting ~~Janner's~~ *his* mind into a dragonfly's mind, to see what ~~the dragonfly~~ *it* saw and feel what ~~the dragonfly~~ *it* felt. ~~Janner~~ *He* imagined the slight turn of a wing that sent ~~the dragonfly~~ *it* zipping across a meadow, whipping left and right, lifting on the wind up over the treetops, or scaling down the craggy drop to the Dark Sea. ~~Janner~~ *He* imagined that if ~~Janner~~ *he* were a dragonfly, ~~Janner~~ *he* would smile while ~~Janner~~ *he* flew (though ~~Janner~~ *he* wasn't sure that dragonflies could smile), because ~~Janner~~ *he* wouldn't have to worry about the ground tripping ~~Janner~~ *him* up. It seemed to Janner that in the last few months ~~Janner~~ *he* had lost control of ~~Janner's~~ *his* limbs; ~~Janner's~~ *his* fingers were longer, ~~Janner's~~ *his* feet were bigger, and ~~Janner's~~ *his* mother had recently said that ~~Janner~~ *he* was all elbows and knees. (modified from page 10)

15.4 Reflective Pronouns

Directions: Use the chart in 15.1 to help you insert the type of pronoun named below the line in each of the following sentences.

Answers will vary. Sample answers are provided.

1. Thomas told ___them___ (personal) not to worry.
2. After doing her own laundry, Mariam washed ___ours___ (possessive).
3. Mrs. Lee calmed ___herself___ (reflexive) as the curtains opened.
4. The singers composed ___themselves___ (reflexive) before the curtains opened.
5. The ball is ___mine___ (possessive).
6. The paper airplane flew by ___itself___ (reflexive) off the table and into the next room.
7. I asked ___her___ (personal) what we should do.
8. In the end, we did it ___ourselves___ (reflexive).
9. Do ___you___ (personal) like coffee?
10. Anthony knows how to laugh at ___himself___ (reflexive).

15.5 Indefinite Pronouns

Directions: Complete each of the following sentences with an indefinite pronoun from the chart on page 425. Make sure it agrees with the verb.

Answers will vary. Sample answers are provided.

1. __Several__ of the children say they will help with the clean-up.

2. The wind blew __everything__ off the table.

3. __Some__ were stranded when the snowstorm closed the highway.

4. __Everyone__ was stranded when the snowstorm closed the highway.

5. My friend is the __one__ wearing a red scarf.

6. The major gave __all__ of the policemen awards for heroism.

7. __Most__ walk instead of taking the bus.

8. I would like to have __some__ with raisins.

Directions: Complete each of the following sentences with a verb form that agrees with the indefinite pronoun.

Answers will vary. Sample answers are provided.

1. No one __is__ home.

2. Everything __was__ in the suitcases.

3. Some of the fans __were__ shouting at the umpire.

4. Neither of us __wants__ to go to bed.

5. All __were__ slow to answer.

6. Everyone __was__ slow to answer.

15.6 Demonstrative Pronouns

Directions: Write sentences using *this*, *these*, *that*, and *those* as demonstrative pronouns and as demonstrative adjectives.

Answers will vary. Sample answers are provided.

This is my mother.

These are wet.

Can you please pass me that?

Are those Grandpa's?

This necklace is pretty.

These towels need to be washed.

Peter loves that magic trick.

Don't forget to pack those flip-flops.

15.7 Can't We All Agree?

Directions: In the sentences below, fill in the blank with a pronoun (or adjective formed from a pronoun) that agrees with the antecedent.

1. Everyone has turned in __his or her__ assignment.
2. The boys left __their__ shoes on the bank and waded into the lake.
3. Mary brought __her__ pet snake to the science fair. __She__ was sure __her__ project would win a blue ribbon.
4. When I saw my brother Jeremy yesterday, I told __him__ that __his__ cat was found alive and well.
5. The bus driver gave the passengers return tickets as __they__ stepped off the bus.

Directions: On the line below each sentence, list three pronouns you can use that agree with the verb.

1. He, she, or it wants to eat.
2. They, we, or you write every day for ten minutes.
3. The clerk gave him, her, or us the bill.
4. I, we, or they go to the post office in the morning.

Directions: The following sentences contain agreement errors. Change the words necessary to make all parts of the sentences agree.

1. We are happy we moved to the city. ~~You~~ We can get anything ~~you~~ we want a short walk away.
2. ~~A teen driver~~ Teen drivers must first pass a written test. Then they take a road test to show they can handle the car properly.
3. ~~A writer~~ Writers should be careful not to confuse their readers.
4. Trevor baked chocolate chip cookies for the party. He told ~~each~~ all of his guests to help ~~ourselves~~ themselves.
5. The scout leader said if we collect enough cans, ~~you~~ we will earn free passes to the park.
6. Most people can improve their writing if ~~you~~ they practice every day.
7. A successful team requires hard work and commitment, but ~~they are~~ it is a great source of enjoyment and friendship.
8. A volunteer at the retirement center must have ~~your~~ his or her application reviewed by the volunteer coordinator first.
9. Food, shelter, and friendship—~~this is~~ these are all I need for happiness.

15.10 Word Sleuth

Directions: A collective noun is a noun used to refer to a group of people or things (such as *crowd*, *flock*, *herd*, or *choir*). Complete the following chart of collective nouns and the groups they describe. You will find a dictionary and the Internet helpful. Ask a parent, teacher, or writing coach to help you with your Internet searches.

Answers will vary. Sample answers are provided.

Collective Nouns	
Collective Noun	**Group**
a **leap** of leopards	a pack of wolves
a **colony** of ants	a pod of dolphins
a **school** of fish	a squad of soldiers
a **team** of cattle	a swarm of bees
a **pride** of lions	a kindle of kittens
a **sloth** of bears	a kaleidoscope of butterflies
a **convocation** of eagles	a herd of rabbits
a **murder** of crows	a host of angels

MODULE 16

16.6 A Close Reading: The Hobbit, Chapter 1

Directions: Read the opening chapter of *The Hobbit*. Use the chart to jot down some of the things you notice in each category.

Answers will vary. Sample answers are provided.

A Close Reading of *The Hobbit*, Chapter 1: "An Unexpected Party"	
Inspect and Analyze	**What I Notice/What I Think**
Title How does the title make readers curious?	It seems unusual for a party to be "unexpected." Usually parties are planned far in advance. This makes me wonder what kind of a party this will be.
Traits of Good Writing	
Ideas What are some of the most creative ideas you find in this chapter? Consider the setting, the characters, and the action.	The way Bilbo's house is constructed (one long hallway through a hill) is creative. So is the way that Gandalf marks Bilbo's door and then removes the mark. The way all of the dwarves have different colored hoods is a creative image. Tolkien contrasts Bilbo's "Tookishness" and his Baggins qualities in a creative way.

A Close Reading of ***The Hobbit***, Chapter 1: "An Unexpected Party"	
Inspect and Analyze	**What I Notice/What I Think**
Organization How does Tolkien organize the events and background information in this chapter?	Tolkien begins with a description of the place and the main character. He gives some background information on Bilbo and his family. Then he begins the action (meeting Gandalf) and continues this action through the end (the meal, the singing, the conversation, all of the dwarves bedding down for the night). Then Tolkien has Bilbo ask for some background information about the gold and the treasure, and Tolkien shares this important information through the character of Thorin as he answers the question. Then he switches back to the action of the story with everybody ordering breakfast and going to sleep.
Traits of Good Writing	
Voice How would you describe the distinct voice Tolkien gives to his narrator?	The narrator's voice is knowledgeable and sympathetic to the characters. It also directly addresses the reader at times, as if the reader has interrupted to ask a question. The narrator really sounds like a storyteller who is relating this tale aloud.
How would you describe Gandalf's distinct voice?	Gandalf seems wise and authoritative. He is kind but in charge.
How would you describe Bilbo's distinct voice?	Bilbo uses words to try to seem like he is capable and smart (even though he is very nervous and unsure). He is also concerned with comfort and details, and he speaks about these things a lot.

A Close Reading of *The Hobbit*, Chapter 1: "An Unexpected Party"	
Inspect and Analyze	**What I Notice/What I Think**
Sentence Structure What are some of the things you notice about Tolkien's sentences?	They are straightforward; Tolkien says what is going on in a way that makes it easy to imagine. They are also descriptive. He chooses words that are specific and vivid.
Word Choice Find examples of specific nouns.	The following are specific nouns: snapdragons, seed-cakes, tassel, clarinets, pine-trees, cradles.
Find examples of vigorous verbs.	The following are vigorous verbs: scuttling, plumped, squeaking, leapt, shuddered, scowled.
Find examples of descriptive adjectives and adverbs.	The following are descriptive adjectives and adverbs: wretched, leathery, uncomfortable, audacious, obstinately, grimly, immovably, immensely.
Conventions How does Tolkien use punctuation to make his sentences easy to read?	He uses dashes, commas, and semicolons to break up long sentences and to connect related thoughts. This makes it easy to know when to pause and for how long.

A Close Reading of *The Hobbit*, Chapter 1: "An Unexpected Party"	
Inspect and Analyze	**What I Notice/What I Think**
Story Elements	
Setting What are some of the things that show you this story is not set in the real world?	There are dwarves, hobbits, and dragons. The houses are built into the sides of hills. There is talk of magic and disappearing.
What kinds of details does Tolkien reveal about the setting?	He describes Bilbo's house, mentioning the round green door with the shiny brass knob. He describes the long tunnel, the paneled walls, and the tiled and carpeted floors. He also tells about the pegs and the polished chairs in the hallway.
Character Development What are some of the ways Tolkien develops the character of Bilbo Baggins?	Tolkien develops Bilbo's character by directly telling us background information about his family, his personality, and his appearance. He also develops Bilbo's character by letting us hear him speak to others (like Gandalf and the dwarves). In addition, sometimes we know Bilbo's thoughts and feelings.

A Close Reading of *The Hobbit*, Chapter 1: "An Unexpected Party"	
Inspect and Analyze	**What I Notice/What I Think**
Story Elements	
What kind of information does he reveal?	Tolkien reveals that Bilbo is from a wealthy family and that although hobbits are usually homebodies, on his mother's side there is a history of adventurousness. He reveals that Bilbo (like all hobbits) is fat, dresses in bright colors, and goes barefoot. He has leathery, hairy feet. He also reveals that Bilbo has mixed feelings about being included in the dwarves' quest. He is nervous and afraid, but he wants to prove that he is worthy of Gandalf's recommendation and that the dwarves are wrong about him.
Inciting Incident What is the inciting incident in this chapter?	The inciting incident is the unexpected party at Bilbo's house where the dwarves reveal that Bilbo has been volunteered (by Gandalf) to accompany them on a dangerous quest.
What is the main problem introduced?	The main problem introduced is that Smaug, a fierce dragon, has stolen much of the dwarves' wealth and they want it back.

16.7 The Hook

Directions: Can you guess the children's story each sentence introduces? Think about why these opening lines are memorable. Record your answers on the following chart.

Answers will vary. Sample answers are provided.

Famous Opening Lines from Children's Books		
Opening Line	**Book**	**Why I Think This Line is Memorable**
"All children, except one, grow up."	Peter Pan	It makes me curious about this child who didn't grow up. That is a surprising characteristic to have!
"In the great green room There was a telephone And a red balloon And a picture of–"	Goodnight Moon	There is alliteration (great green) and consonance (green, telephone, balloon), so this sentence is pleasing to the ear.
"The sun did not shine. It was too wet to play. So we sat in the house All that cold, cold, wet day."	The Cat in the Hat	The rhyming is fun to read aloud. It also sounds like the problem of being stuck inside on a rainy day may lead to adventures.

Famous Opening Lines from Children's Books		
Opening Line	**Book**	**Why I Think This Line is Memorable**
"When Mary Lennox was sent to Misselthwaite Manor to live with her uncle, everybody said she was the most disagreeable-looking child ever seen."	The Secret Garden	The author saying that everybody said Mary was "disagreeable-looking" is shocking and kind of funny. It is also surprising to hear of a child who has to go live with an uncle. This opening line makes me want to know more about who Mary is, why she had to go live with her uncle, and who these critical people are who think she is so disagreeable-looking.
"Here is Edward Bear, coming downstairs now, bump, bump, bump, on the back of his head, behind Christopher Robin."	Winnie-the-Pooh	The "bump, bump, bump" part is fun to read because it makes me able to hear Edward Bear being dragged downstairs. The structure of the sentence is almost poetic and symmetrical, starting with a name (Edward Bear), "bump, bump, bump" in the middle, and then ending with another name (Christopher Robin).

Famous Opening Lines from Children's Books		
Opening Line	**Book**	**Why I Think This Line is Memorable**
"The night Max wore his wolf suit and made mischief of one kind and another his mother called him 'WILD THING!' and Max said 'I'LL EAT YOU UP!' so he was sent to bed without eating anything."	Where the Wild Things Are	This line is memorable because so much happens. Max's costume, his mischief, his fight with his mother, and his punishment all show up in one sentence! It is also memorable because Max sounds like an interesting character with a wild imagination.
"There was a boy called Eustace Clarence Scrubb, and he almost deserved it."	The Voyage of the Dawn Treader	This opening line is humorous, drawing attention to an unpleasant name and also hinting that the boy is unpleasant too.
"Marley was dead, to begin with."	A Christmas Carol	This line is abrupt. People don't usually come out and say that someone is dead so bluntly. It seems like a strange way to begin a story.

Famous Opening Lines from Children's Books		
Opening Line	**Book**	**Why I Think This Line is Memorable**
"In an old house in Paris that was covered with vines lived twelve little girls in two straight lines."	Madeline	The meter and rhyme of this line are pleasing to the ear. It also paints a vivid picture in my mind of the old house, the vines, and the two straight lines of girls.
"In the light of the moon a little egg lay on a leaf."	The Very Hungry Caterpillar	The alliteration makes the sentence fun to read (light, little, lay, leaf). It is also simple (most words are just one syllable) and sounds like a setup for something exciting to happen (the egg hatching maybe).

Unit 4 Review

Directions: You may write your answers to the questions below in the space provided, or you can talk about these questions with a parent, teacher, or writing coach. You can also look over all the information in the modules you have completed to help you decide on your answers. Use the unit review to help you master the writing tips and tricks you learned about in these modules.

Answers will vary. Sample answers are provided.

1. List some of the things writers do during the planning stages of a story. (4 points)

During the planning stages, writers think about their intended audience and what will appeal to this audience. They brainstorm ideas for their characters, their settings (both when and where a story will occur), and problems that will need to be resolved. Sometimes they plan what will happen in each stage of the plot.

2. Why is it important for writers to know a lot about the setting before they begin to write a story? (4 points)

It is important to know a lot about the setting because often the setting impacts the characters and the action. The setting is also a big way that writers paint a vivid picture for their readers, so it is worthwhile to really think through what details will make it come to life.

3. Why do you think writers write best when they know their readers well? (4 points)

When writers know their readers well, they can tailor their writing to those particular readers. They can imagine what will entertain and delight them rather than just writing for a general audience (or for no one). They can imagine what kind of characters and action their unique audience will find appealing. They can try to connect with the sense of humor their intended audience may have.

4. How can studying the rubric during the writing process help you write a more successful story? (4 points)

Studying the rubric is a great way to check whether I am remembering all of my goals for my story. It might remind me that I have not written an opening hook or that I have been switching between different points of view. I can fix these things as I go along rather than not noticing the problems until after I have finished. The rubric can be like a road map and remind me of the plot structure I want to use, keeping me from going off on tangents that I didn't mean to include.

5. Explain what happens in the following stages of a plot: (8 points)

Exposition – This is where we learn about the major characters, the setting (both time and place), and any needed background information.

Inciting incident – This is where the main conflict or problem is introduced. This is the event that sets the rest of the action in motion.

Rising action – This is where the problem gets more intense due to other complicating events. The suspense rises.

Climax – This is where we know that the problem is about to be resolved because the tension has reached its highest point.

Falling action – Here we see the problems starting to be resolved and the suspense decreasing.

Resolution – This is where the conflict totally ends and we see how the characters were impacted by what happened in the story.

6. Describe two points of view a writer can use to tell a story. List some of the advantages and disadvantages of each. (4 points)

A writer can use first-person point of view or third-person point of view. In first-person point of view, the story is told from the perspective of the main character and the narrator refers to himself using first-person pronouns. The readers can see what he is thinking and feeling as well as what he is saying and doing. In third-person point of view, the narrator does not refer to himself directly but uses third-person pronouns.

An advantage of a first-person point of view is that it tends to cause readers to deeply empathize with the main character. Because readers are intimately aware of all the main character thinks and feels, they care a lot about what happens in the story. This keeps them reading.

A disadvantage of a first-person point of view is that it can be challenging to figure out how to reveal important events that take place without the main character present. The writer always has to be thinking about how to reveal important information to the narrator so that the readers know it too. Another disadvantage is that a writer is limited to one perspective (the narrator's).

An advantage of a third-person point of view is that the writer can show the readers what is happening at different times and places. The writer can portray scenes that involve different characters without always having to make sure the main character is present. The writer can also give important background information without having to involve the main character's thoughts or conversations.

A disadvantage of a third-person point of view (particularly third-person objective and third-person omniscient) is that it is more difficult to connect readers to the intimate thoughts and feelings of a particular character.

7. What are some common problems with pronouns you should avoid when you write? (4 points)

A common problem with pronouns is unclear or missing antecedents. Another problem is pronouns that don't agree with their antecedents or verbs. They must agree in person, number, and gender.

8. Describe how writers can show but not tell readers about their characters and settings. (4 points)

Writers can show information about their characters through what those characters say and do. Rather than writing "Steven was brave," a writer can show Steven doing something brave in the face of danger. Writers can also include details about their characters within the action rather than stopping the action to tell something. For example, it is more interesting to write "Heidi blinked her sea-green eyes in surprise" than "Heidi had green eyes." In addition, writers can give specific details. Rather than saying "John looked like a typical grandpa," a writer can show John's gray hair, his corduroy jacket, his gold-rimmed glasses, and his wrinkled skin.

Writers can do that same thing with setting. They can describe what a region looks like as the action is occurring in it. They can also include vivid details (like "sparkling blue water and milky white sand") rather than just telling the readers "it was a nice beach."

9. How can writers vivify the voices of their narrators and characters? (4 points)

Writers can vivify the voices of their narrators and characters through word choice. They can pick words for their connotative values, choosing words that inspire certain feelings or impressions. They can also use punctuation to reveal the emotion and cadence with which their narrators and characters speak.

Unit 1 Student's Rubric

Rubric Point System:

5 points – This is the best I've ever done.

4 points – This is a strength in this piece.

3 points – I improved here in this assignment.

2 points – I remembered to pay attention to this.

1 point – I need to improve in this area.

Student's Rubric for "Into the Wild"	
Traits of Good Writing	Points Earned
Ideas • I chose my topic through a systematic process.	
• I collected the information in my report from reliable and verifiable sources.	
• My sentences contain facts and interesting details from my research.	
• I properly documented the words and ideas of others in my report.	
• I paraphrased and summarized my research in my own words.	
• I included some of my own ideas and experiences that show what I learned.	
• I included illustrations that provide additional information for my readers.	
Organization • I presented my research in a question-and-answer format.	
• I organized my report by related topics.	
• I introduced each topic with an engaging question that requires several sentences to answer fully.	
• I organized the questions and answers in a logical way.	
• The information in each answer is related to the corresponding question.	
Sentence Structure • All my sentences are complete thoughts.*	

Continued on next page »

Unit 1 Student's Rubric

Student's Rubric for "Into the Wild"	
Traits of Good Writing	Points Earned
Word Choice • All my nouns are as specific as they can be.*	
• I used vigorous verbs to describe the action.*	
• I chose adjectives and adverbs that add descriptive details.*	
• I used interrogative adverbs and interrogative pronouns to create questions about my animal.	
Conventions • I properly documented my sources in the body of my report.	
• I properly documented my sources in the bibliography.	
• I properly alphabetized my list of sources in the bibliography.	
• I followed the rules for capitalization carefully, especially in my titles.	
• I punctuated my direct quotations correctly.	
• I punctuated the end of each sentence correctly, including my questions.*	
• I checked to make sure all my words are spelled correctly.	
Total	

Unit 1: 120 points possible

Rubric Point System:

5 points – This is the best I've ever done.

4 points – This is a strength in this piece.

3 points – I improved here in this assignment.

2 points – I remembered to pay attention to this.

1 point – I need to improve in this area.

Unit 2 Student's Rubric

Rubric Point System:

5 points – This is the best I've ever done.

4 points – This is a strength in this piece.

3 points – I improved here in this assignment.

2 points – I remembered to pay attention to this.

1 point – I need to improve in this area.

Student's Rubric for "Making the Case"	
Traits of Good Writing	**Points Earned**
Ideas • I proposed a destination for a dream vacation that all my travel companions accepted.	
• I based my argument on facts that can be verified and logical reasoning.	
• I stated my thesis in my introduction.	
• I developed my ideas with reasons, facts, examples, and details.	
Organization • I included an introduction, body paragraphs, and a conclusion in my essay.	
• I created a hook in the introduction that engages my readers' interest and attention.	
• I used an organizational pattern that is clear to my readers.	
• Each paragraph has a central idea that is fully supported.	
• Each sentence fulfills a clear purpose in the paragraph.	
• My conclusion seals the deal with a convincing finish to my argument and links back to my introduction.	

Continued on next page »

Unit 2 Student's Rubric

Student's Rubric for "Making the Case"	
Traits of Good Writing	Points Earned
Voice • I inserted my personality into my writing with punctuation and word choices that show my emotions.	
• I used a consistent tone to address my readers.	
Sentence Structure • I used a few short sentences to help me add emotion to my voice.	
• I used transitions to connect my ideas or signal my readers about what is coming next.*	
• I can identify some of the basic sentence parts and the jobs they perform in many of my sentences.	
Word Choice • All my nouns are as specific as they can be.*	
• I used vigorous verbs to describe the action.*	
• I chose adjectives and adverbs that add descriptive details.*	
Conventions • I followed the rules for capitalization carefully.*	
• I punctuated the end of each sentence correctly, including my questions.*	
• I checked to make sure all my words are spelled correctly.	
Total	

Unit 1: 105 points possible

Rubric Point System:

5 points – This is the best I've ever done.

4 points – This is a strength in this piece.

3 points – I improved here in this assignment.

2 points – I remembered to pay attention to this.

1 point – I need to improve in this area.

Unit 3 Student's Rubric

Rubric Point System:

5 points – This is the best I've ever done.

4 points – This is a strength in this piece.

3 points – I improved here in this assignment.

2 points – I remembered to pay attention to this.

1 point – I need to improve in this area.

Student's Rubric for Acrostic Poem	
Traits of Good Writing (Poetry)	Points Earned
Ideas • The poem is based on a word or phrase that is important to me.	
• Each line defines, describes, or is related to the word or phrase the acrostic spells.	
Organization • A word in each line of my poem contains a letter in the acrostic.	
Sound and Rhythm • I used the sound device of rhyme in my acrostic poem.	
• I used other sound devices such as alliteration, assonance, and consonance.	
• I arranged my words so that they create a regular meter of stressed and unstressed syllables and words.	
Sentence Structure • I used a few short sentences to help me add emotion to my voice.	
Word Choice • All my nouns are as specific as they can be.*	
• I used vigorous verbs to describe the action.*	
• I chose adjectives and adverbs that add descriptive details.*	
Conventions • I used punctuation to show readers how the poem should be read.	
• I checked to make sure all my words are spelled correctly.	
Total	

Acrostic Poem: 60 points possible

Unit 3 Student's Rubric

Student's Rubric for Lyric Poem	
Traits of Good Writing (Poetry)	**Points Earned**
Ideas • The poem is based on a memory or experience that is important to me.	
• I expressed how I feel about this memory.	
• I expressed what this memory means to me.	
• I used figures of speech (such as similes and metaphors) to add layers of meaning.	
Organization • My lyric poem has an opening that gives readers clues about where and when this memory takes place.	
• In the middle of the poem, I developed the imagery and action with details about what I can see, hear, feel, taste, or smell.	
• The closing of the poem expresses what this memory means to me now.	
Sound and Rhythm • I used the sound device of rhyme in my lyric poem.	
• I used other sound devices such as alliteration, assonance, and consonance.	
• I arranged my words so that they create a regular meter of stressed and unstressed syllables and words.	

Rubric Point System:

5 points – This is the best I've ever done.

4 points – This is a strength in this piece.

3 points – I improved here in this assignment.

2 points – I remembered to pay attention to this.

1 point – I need to improve in this area.

Unit 3 Student's Rubric

Rubric Point System:

5 points – This is the best I've ever done.

4 points – This is a strength in this piece.

3 points – I improved here in this assignment.

2 points – I remembered to pay attention to this.

1 point – I need to improve in this area.

Student's Rubric for Lyric Poem	
Traits of Good Writing (Poetry)	**Points Earned**
Word Choice • All my nouns are as specific as they can be.*	
• I used vigorous verbs to describe the action.*	
• I chose adjectives and adverbs that add descriptive details.*	
• I included words for their connotative values.	
Conventions • I used punctuation to show readers how the poem should be read.	
• I checked to make sure all my words are spelled correctly.	
Total	

Lyric Poem: 80 points possible

Unit 3 Student's Rubric

Student's Rubric for Haiku	
Traits of Good Writing (Poetry)	**Points Earned**
Ideas • The subject of each poem is limited to a single, striking image or experience.	
• I described the striking image or experience in a surprising way.	
Organization • I organized my poem with the traditional number of lines.	
• I organized my poem with the approximate number of syllables.	
Sound and Rhythm • I selected words with vowel sounds that add to the musicality of the poem.	
• I arranged my words so that they create a regular meter of stressed and unstressed syllables and words.	
Word Choice • All my nouns are as specific as they can be.*	
• I used vigorous verbs to describe the action.*	
• I chose adjectives and adverbs that add descriptive details.*	
• I included words for their connotative values.	
Conventions • I used punctuation to show readers how the poem should be read.	
• I checked to make sure all my words are spelled correctly.	
Total	

Haiku: 60 points possible

Rubric Point System:

5 points – This is the best I've ever done.

4 points – This is a strength in this piece.

3 points – I improved here in this assignment.

2 points – I remembered to pay attention to this.

1 point – I need to improve in this area.

Unit 3 Student's Rubric

Rubric Point System:

5 points – This is the best I've ever done.

4 points – This is a strength in this piece.

3 points – I improved here in this assignment.

2 points – I remembered to pay attention to this.

1 point – I need to improve in this area.

Student's Rubric for Cinquain	
Traits of Good Writing (Poetry)	**Points Earned**
Ideas • The subject of each poem is limited to a single, striking image or experience.	
• I described the striking image or experience in a surprising way.	
Organization • I organized my poem with the traditional number of lines.	
• I organized my poem with the approximate number of syllables.	
Sound and Rhythm • I selected words with vowel sounds that add to the musicality of the poem.	
• I arranged my words so that they create a regular meter of stressed and unstressed syllables and words.	
Word Choice • All my nouns are as specific as they can be.*	
• I used vigorous verbs to describe the action.*	
• I chose adjectives and adverbs that add descriptive details.*	
• I included words for their connotative values.	
Conventions • I used punctuation to show readers how the poem should be read.	
• I checked to make sure all my words are spelled correctly.	
Total	

Cinquain: 60 points possible

Unit 4 Student's Rubric

Student's Rubric for "A Fantastical Tale of Extraordinary Exploits"	
Traits of Good Writing	**Points Earned**
Ideas • I created a fantastical setting.	
• I included details and dialogue that reveal the setting to my readers at the beginning of the story.	
• I developed a plot with a main problem that is not too big or too small to be introduced and resolved in my story.	
• I created a main character that my readers care about.	
• I created a cast of characters that includes talking animals or imaginary creatures.	
Organization • I created an opening hook that engages my readers' interest and attention.	
• I included an inciting incident that introduces the main problem.	
• Each sentence fulfills a clear purpose in the paragraph.	
• My plot includes exposition, rising action, climax, falling action, and resolution.	
Voice • I created a narrator with a distinct voice.	
• I used a consistent point of view throughout the story.	
• I gave my major characters distinct voices that reveal their character traits.	

Rubric Point System:

5 points – This is the best I've ever done.

4 points – This is a strength in this piece.

3 points – I improved here in this assignment.

2 points – I remembered to pay attention to this.

1 point – I need to improve in this area.

Continued on next page »

Unit 4 Student's Rubric

Rubric Point System:

5 points – This is the best I've ever done.

4 points – This is a strength in this piece.

3 points – I improved here in this assignment.

2 points – I remembered to pay attention to this.

1 point – I need to improve in this area.

Student's Rubric for "A Fantastical Tale of Extraordinary Exploits"	
Traits of Good Writing	**Points Earned**
• I chose words for their connotations and used punctuation to add meaning, emotion, and cadence to my narrator's and other characters' voices.	
Sentence Structure • I used transitions to connect my ideas or signal my readers about what is coming next.*	
• I varied the length of my sentences to show when my characters are speaking slowly and when they are speaking more quickly.	
Word Choice • All my nouns are as specific as they can be.*	
• I used vigorous verbs to describe the action.*	
• I chose adjectives and adverbs that add descriptive details.*	
• The antecedents of pronouns are clear and nearby.	
Conventions • I followed the rules for capitalization carefully.*	
• I properly punctuated the dialogue between characters.*	
• My pronouns are in agreement with other parts of the sentence.	
• I checked to make sure all my words are spelled correctly.	
Total	

Unit 4: 115 points possible

Unit 1 Reviewer's Rubric

4.9 Reviewer's Rubric: "Into the Wild"	
Traits of Good Writing	**Points Earned**
Ideas • The writer chose a topic through a systematic process.	
• The writer collected the information in the report from reliable and verifiable sources.	
• The writer's sentences contain facts and interesting details from the research.	
• The writer paraphrased and summarized the research in his or her own words.	
• The writer included some of his or her own ideas and experiences that show what he or she learned.	
• The writer included illustrations that provide additional information for the readers.	
Organization • The writer presented the research in a question-and-answer format.	
• The writer organized the report by related topics.	
• The writer introduced each topic with an engaging question that requires several sentences to answer fully.	
• The writer organized the questions and answers in a logical way.	
• The information in each answer is related to the corresponding question.	

Rubric Point System:

5 points – This is the best I've ever done.

4 points – This is a strength in this piece.

3 points – I improved here in this assignment.

2 points – I remembered to pay attention to this.

1 point – I need to improve in this area.

Continued on next page »

Unit 1 Reviewer's Rubric

Rubric Point System:

5 points – This is the best I've ever done.

4 points – This is a strength in this piece.

3 points – I improved here in this assignment.

2 points – I remembered to pay attention to this.

1 point – I need to improve in this area.

4.9 Reviewer's Rubric: "Into the Wild"	
Traits of Good Writing	**Points Earned**
Sentence Structure • All the sentences are complete thoughts.	
Word Choice • All the nouns are as specific as they can be.	
• The writer used vigorous verbs to describe the action.	
• The writer chose adjectives and adverbs that add descriptive details.	
• The writer used interrogative adverbs and interrogative pronouns to create questions about the animal.	
Conventions • The writer properly documented the sources in the body of the report.	
• The writer properly documented the sources in the bibliography.	
• The writer properly alphabetized the list of sources in the bibliography.	
• The writer followed the rules for capitalization carefully, especially in titles.	
• The writer punctuated direct quotations correctly.	
• The writer punctuated the end of each sentence correctly, including the questions.	
• All the words are spelled correctly.	
Total	

Unit 1: 120 points possible

Unit 2 Reviewer's Rubric

8.13 Reviewer's Rubric: "Making the Case"	
Traits of Good Writing	**Points Earned**
Ideas • The writer proposed a destination for a dream vacation that all the travel companions accepted.	
• The writer based the argument on facts that can be verified and logical reasoning.	
• The writer stated the thesis in the introduction.	
• The writer developed his or her ideas with reasons, facts, examples, and details.	
Organization • The writer included an introduction, body paragraphs, and a conclusion in the essay.	
• The writer created a hook in the introduction that engages the readers' interest and attention.	
• The writer used an organizational pattern that is clear to the readers.	
• Each paragraph has a central idea that is fully supported.	
• Each sentence fulfills a clear purpose in the paragraph.	
• The conclusion seals the deal with a convincing finish to the argument and links back to the introduction.	
Voice • The writer inserted his or her personality into the writing with punctuation and word choices that show his or her emotions.	

Rubric Point System:

5 points – This is the best I've ever done.

4 points – This is a strength in this piece.

3 points – I improved here in this assignment.

2 points – I remembered to pay attention to this.

1 point – I need to improve in this area.

Continued on next page »

Unit 2 Reviewer's Rubric

8.13 Reviewer's Rubric: "Making the Case"	
Traits of Good Writing	**Points Earned**
• The writer used a consistent tone to address the readers.	
Sentence Structure • The writer used a few short sentences to help add emotion to his or her voice.	
• The writer used transitions to connect ideas or signal the readers about what is coming next.	
• The writer can identify some of the basic sentence parts and the jobs they perform in many of the sentences.	
Word Choice • All the nouns are as specific as they can be.	
• The writer used vigorous verbs to describe the action.	
• The writer chose adjectives and adverbs that add descriptive details.	
Conventions • The writer followed the rules for capitalization carefully.	
• The writer punctuated the end of each sentence correctly, including the questions.	
• All the words are spelled correctly.	
Total	

Unit 1: 105 points possible

Rubric Point System:

5 points – This is the best I've ever done.

4 points – This is a strength in this piece.

3 points – I improved here in this assignment.

2 points – I remembered to pay attention to this.

1 point – I need to improve in this area.

Unit 3 Reviewer's Rubric

12.10 Reviewer's Rubric: Acrostic Poem	
Traits of Good Writing	**Points Earned**
Ideas • The poem is based on a word or phrase that is important to the writer.	
• Each line defines, describes, or is related to the word or phrase the acrostic spells.	
Organization • A word in each line of the poem contains a letter in the acrostic.	
Sound and Rhythm • The writer used the sound device of rhyme in the acrostic poem.	
• The writer used other sound devices such as alliteration, assonance, and consonance.	
• The writer arranged the words so that they create a regular meter of stressed and unstressed syllables and words.	
Sentence Structure • The writer used a few short sentences to help add emotion to his or her voice.	
Word Choice • All the nouns are as specific as they can be.	
• The writer used vigorous verbs to describe the action.	
• The writer chose adjectives and adverbs that add descriptive details.	
Conventions • The writer used punctuation to show readers how the poem should be read.	
• All the words are spelled correctly.	
Total	

Acrostic Poem: 60 points possible

Rubric Point System:

5 points – This is the best I've ever done.

4 points – This is a strength in this piece.

3 points – I improved here in this assignment.

2 points – I remembered to pay attention to this.

1 point – I need to improve in this area.

Unit 3 Reviewer's Rubric

Rubric Point System:

5 points – This is the best I've ever done.

4 points – This is a strength in this piece.

3 points – I improved here in this assignment.

2 points – I remembered to pay attention to this.

1 point – I need to improve in this area.

12.10 Reviewer's Rubric: Lyric Poem	
Traits of Good Writing	**Points Earned**
Ideas • The poem is based on a memory or experience that is important to the writer.	
• The writer expressed how he or she feels about this memory.	
• The writer expressed what this memory means to him or her.	
• The writer used figures of speech (such as similes and metaphors) to add layers of meaning.	
Organization • The lyric poem has an opening that gives readers clues about where and when this memory takes place.	
• In the middle of the poem, the writer developed the imagery and action with details about what he or she can see, hear, feel, taste, and smell.	
• The closing of the poem expresses what this memory means to the writer now.	
Sound and Rhythm • The writer used the sound device of rhyme in the lyric poem.	
• The writer used other sound devices such as alliteration, assonance, and consonance.	
• The writer arranged the words so that they create a regular meter of stressed and unstressed syllables and words.	

Continued on next page »

Unit 3 Reviewer's Rubric

12.10 Reviewer's Rubric: Lyric Poem	
Traits of Good Writing	**Points Earned**
Word Choice • All the nouns are as specific as they can be.	
• The writer used vigorous verbs to describe the action.	
• The writer chose adjectives and adverbs that add descriptive details.	
• The writer included words for their connotative values.	
Conventions • The writer used punctuation to show readers how the poem should be read.	
• All the words are spelled correctly.	
Total	

Lyric Poem: 80 points possible

Rubric Point System:

5 points – This is the best I've ever done.

4 points – This is a strength in this piece.

3 points – I improved here in this assignment.

2 points – I remembered to pay attention to this.

1 point – I need to improve in this area.

Unit 3 Reviewer's Rubric

Rubric Point System:

5 points – This is the best I've ever done.

4 points – This is a strength in this piece.

3 points – I improved here in this assignment.

2 points – I remembered to pay attention to this.

1 point – I need to improve in this area.

12.10 Reviewer's Rubric: Haiku	
Traits of Good Writing	**Points Earned**
Ideas • The subject of each poem is limited to a single, striking image or experience.	
• The writer described the striking image or experience in a surprising way.	
Organization • The writer organized the poem with the traditional number of lines.	
• The writer organized the poem with the approximate number of syllables.	
Sound and Rhythm • The writer selected words with vowel sounds that add to the musicality of the poem.	
• The writer arranged the words so that they create a regular meter of stressed and unstressed syllables and words.	
Word Choice • All the nouns are as specific as they can be.	
• The writer used vigorous verbs to describe the action.	
• The writer chose adjectives and adverbs that add descriptive details.	
• The writer included words for their connotative values.	
Conventions • The writer used punctuation to show readers how the poem should be read.	
• All the words are spelled correctly.	
Total	

Haiku: 60 points possible

Unit 3 Reviewer's Rubric

12.10 Reviewer's Rubric: Cinquain	
Traits of Good Writing	**Points Earned**
Ideas • The subject of each poem is limited to a single, striking image or experience.	
• The writer described the striking image or experience in a surprising way.	
Organization • The writer organized the poem with the traditional number of lines.	
• The writer organized the poem with the approximate number of syllables.	
Sound and Rhythm • The writer selected words with vowel sounds that add to the musicality of the poem.	
• The writer arranged the words so that they create a regular meter of stressed and unstressed syllables and words.	
Word Choice • All the nouns are as specific as they can be.	
• The writer used vigorous verbs to describe the action.	
• The writer chose adjectives and adverbs that add descriptive details.	
• The writer included words for their connotative values.	
Conventions • The writer used punctuation to show readers how the poem should be read.	
• All the words are spelled correctly.	
Total	

Cinquain: 60 points possible

Rubric Point System:

5 points – This is the best I've ever done.

4 points – This is a strength in this piece.

3 points – I improved here in this assignment.

2 points – I remembered to pay attention to this.

1 point – I need to improve in this area.

Unit 4 Reviewer's Rubric

Rubric Point System:

5 points – This is the best I've ever done.

4 points – This is a strength in this piece.

3 points – I improved here in this assignment.

2 points – I remembered to pay attention to this.

1 point – I need to improve in this area.

16.10 Reviewer's Rubric: "A Fantastical Tale of Extraordinary Exploits"	
Traits of Good Writing	**Points Earned**
Ideas • The writer created a fantastical setting.	
• The writer included details and dialogue that reveal the setting to readers at the beginning of the story.	
• The writer developed a plot with a main problem that is not too big or too small to be introduced and resolved in the story.	
• The writer created a main character that readers care about.	
• The writer created a cast of characters that includes talking animals or imaginary creatures.	
Organization • The writer created an opening hook that engages readers' interest and attention.	
• The writer included an inciting incident that introduces the main problem.	
• Each sentence fulfills a clear purpose in the paragraph.	
• The plot includes exposition, rising action, climax, falling action, and resolution.	
Voice • The writer created a narrator with a distinct voice.	
• The writer used a consistent point of view throughout the story.	
• The writer gave the major characters distinct voices that reveal their character traits.	

Continued on next page »

Unit 4 Reviewer's Rubric

16.10 Reviewer's Rubric: "A Fantastical Tale of Extraordinary Exploits"	
Traits of Good Writing	**Points Earned**
• The writer chose words for their connotations and used punctuation to add meaning, emotion, and cadence to the narrator's and other characters' voices.	
Sentence Structure • The writer used transitions to connect ideas or signal readers about what is coming next.	
• The writer varied the length of the sentences to show when the characters are speaking slowly and when they are speaking more quickly.	
Word Choice • All the nouns are as specific as they can be.	
• The writer used vigorous verbs to describe the action.	
• The writer chose adjectives and adverbs that add descriptive details.	
• The antecedents of pronouns are clear and nearby.	
Conventions • The writer followed the rules for capitalization carefully.	
• The writer properly punctuated the dialogue between characters.	
• The pronouns are in agreement with other parts of the sentence.	
• All the words are spelled correctly	
Total	

Unit 4: 115 points possible

Rubric Point System:

5 points – This is the best I've ever done.

4 points – This is a strength in this piece.

3 points – I improved here in this assignment.

2 points – I remembered to pay attention to this.

1 point – I need to improve in this area.

Checklist for Module 1

Directions: When you have completed a task, make a ✔ in the "Done" column. Ask a parent, teacher, or writing coach to award you points for each task using the checklist point system. Fill in the points you have earned on the Journeyman Log in the appendix.

Checklist Point System:

1–6 points may be awarded by a parent, teacher, or writing coach for each task completed. Here are the recommended guidelines:

6 – exemplary in quality *and* effort

5 – exemplary in either quality *or* effort

4 – acceptable in quality *and* effort

3 – acceptable in either quality *or* effort

2 – needs improvement in quality *and* effort

1 – incomplete

Tasks	Done ✔	Points Earned
1.4 Get Your Gear • On the lines provided, note how you will keep track of your research.		
• Include details about how you will label your notebook or file folders and where you will store your notes so you won't lose them.		
• Discuss your plans with a parent, teacher, or writing coach.		
1.7 Test 1: Who Said It? • Discuss the kinds of occupations, education, or experiences that would help a person become an expert about different types of wildlife in your state with a parent, teacher, or writing coach.		
• Write your ideas on the lines provided.		
1.10 Types of Websites • With the help of a parent, teacher, or writing coach, conduct an Internet search for information about your state capital.		
• Conduct several searches using different keywords and phrases, with and without quotation marks.		
• Try to find at least one site that fits each type of website listed.		
• Write the name of the site and the URL on the line provided.		
• Use this exercise to talk about the clues that tell you which sites are safe and which sites may not be. Discuss how to tell the type of site a URL will link you to from the description provided in the search results.		

Continued on next page »

Tasks	Done ✔	Points Earned
1.11 Test Drive • Before you begin your research, estimate the number of animal species in your state. Write the number on the line provided.		
• With the help of a parent, teacher, or writing coach, use the Internet to research the different species of wildlife that live in your state. Use keywords similar to the ones used in 1.9 by the author of the expert model. Search without and with quotation marks around your keywords.		
• Identify which sites retrieved by your search you should investigate further.		
• List some of the sites that provide the best information about the species of animals that live in your state. Follow the guidelines in 1.7 to make sure the sites you select are reliable sources of information.		
• From the sites you investigated further, come up with a new estimate of how many different species of animals live in your state. Write that approximate number on the line provided.		
1.13 Investigate This • Choose the category you are most interested in learning more about for this project.		
• With the help of a parent, teacher, or writing coach, find a reliable website that lists your state wildlife in the category you chose. Use the My State Animals chart to record the names of all the animals in your chosen category.		
• Confirm your list using two or more reliable sources on the Internet.		
• Circle any animal on your list experts do not agree on.		
• Record the reliable sources you used on the lines provided.		

Continued on next page »

Checklist Point System:

1–6 points may be awarded by a parent, teacher, or writing coach for each task completed. Here are the recommended guidelines:

6 – exemplary in quality *and* effort

5 – exemplary in either quality *or* effort

4 – acceptable in quality *and* effort

3 – acceptable in either quality *or* effort

2 – needs improvement in quality *and* effort

1 – incomplete

Checklist Point System:

1–6 points may be awarded by a parent, teacher, or writing coach for each task completed. Here are the recommended guidelines:

6 – exemplary in quality *and* effort

5 – exemplary in either quality *or* effort

4 – acceptable in quality *and* effort

3 – acceptable in either quality *or* effort

2 – needs improvement in quality *and* effort

1 – incomplete

Tasks	Done ✔	Points Earned
1.14 Where the Wild Things Are • With the help of a parent, teacher, or writing coach, list the potential places to visit on the Potential Field Trips chart.		
• Note each location's hours and fees.		
• Note the animals you will be able to research if you visit and the kinds of information you will find.		
1.15 The Sandbox • Imagine the kinds of information scientists might report about you if they decided to study you in your natural habitat (in your home with your family).		
• Answer the suggested questions or others you find more interesting in your science report.		
• Organize your report using the Q&A format. Ask and answer at least four questions. Share with family and friends.		
1.16 Word Sleuth • Create an animal alphabet with animal names that are new to you.		
• Look up a picture of each animal on the Internet or in a reference book.		
• Share your animal alphabet with a younger sibling or friend.		
1.17 Revisit: Writer's Questions • Discuss your answers to the Writer's Questions from the beginning of the module with a parent, teacher, or writing coach.		
Total		

Module 1:180 points possible

Checklist for Module 2

Directions: When you have completed a task, make a ✔ in the "Done" column. Ask a parent, teacher, or writing coach to award you points for each task using the checklist point system. Fill in the points you have earned on the JOURNEYMAN LOG in the appendix.

Tasks	Done ✔	Points Earned
2.3 Choosing a Topic: Short-List It • List the three animals that interest you most after conducting your preliminary research on the Internet and reviewing the field trip opportunities nearby on the SHORT-LISTED TOPICS CHART.		
• Explain why you are short-listing each animal.		
2.4 Library Research • Schedule a trip to the library to collect information for your science report.		
• Make an appointment with a staff member who can show you how to find what you need.		
• Before you go, familiarize yourself with your library's website.		
2.6 Research the Resources • On the RESOURCES AT MY LIBRARY CHART, list the best resources at your local library that may help you complete this assignment.		
2.7 Is It Reliable? Is It Verifiable? • On the lines provided, list three resources at your local library you believe provide reliable information.		
• Briefly describe why you think the author or publisher of each resource is trustworthy.		
2.8 And the Winner Is . . . • Briefly answer the questions on the lines provided.		

Checklist Point System:

1–6 points may be awarded by a parent, teacher, or writing coach for each task completed. Here are the recommended guidelines:

6 – exemplary in quality *and* effort

5 – exemplary in either quality *or* effort

4 – acceptable in quality *and* effort

3 – acceptable in either quality *or* effort

2 – needs improvement in quality *and* effort

1 – incomplete

Continued on next page »

Checklist Point System:

1–6 points may be awarded by a parent, teacher, or writing coach for each task completed. Here are the recommended guidelines:

6 – exemplary in quality *and* effort

5 – exemplary in either quality *or* effort

4 – acceptable in quality *and* effort

3 – acceptable in either quality *or* effort

2 – needs improvement in quality *and* effort

1 – incomplete

Tasks	Done ✔	Points Earned
• Discuss your responses with a parent, teacher, or writing coach.		
• Write the name of the animal you will research further for this assignment.		
• Paste or draw a picture of your animal in the margin.		
• Explain why you have decided to investigate this animal.		
• Share your decision with a parent, teacher, or writing coach.		
2.10 Study Strategy 1: Get Organized—Get Smart! • Organize a space devoted to this research project.		
• Choose the reliable sources you will use and put them in your study area.		
• Decide the best order for studying your resources.		
• Decide where you will store your notes. Put your note-taking supplies in your study area too.		
• Make sure you have enough light in your study space. Take a photo of your completed study area.		
2.11 Study Strategy 2: Write to Learn • Study the tables of contents and indexes for the books you collected, plus the topics covered on the websites you located.		
• Create a list of topics to help you organize what you learn during your study sessions.		
• Write your list in pencil so you can revise it to accommodate more information. Be prepared to change this list and add to it as you read.		

Continued on next page »

Tasks	Done ✔	Points Earned
2.17 Workout Record • Take at least three days to study the resources you collected.		
• Make a record of your study habits. Put a check mark beside each study strategy you use each day of your study session.		
2.18 Find an Expert • Ask a parent, teacher, or writing coach to help you schedule a field trip and an appointment to talk to an expert about your wildlife project.		
• Record the location, date, and time for your field trip on the lines provided.		
2.19 Take Your Field Trip • Take your field trip.		
• Interview an expert about your wildlife topic.		
• After you complete your field trip, briefly describe where you went, what you saw, and what you learned in your interview.		
2.20 Word Sleuth • As you read about your chosen animal, add new vocabulary words, especially science-related terms, and their definitions to the chart.		
• Include the part of speech that matches the definition. Try to fill the chart with new terms.		
2.21 Revisit: Writer's Questions • Discuss your answers to the WRITER'S QUESTIONS from the beginning of the module with a parent, teacher, or writing coach.		
Total		

Module 2: 192 points possible, plus six points for each check mark on 2.17 WORKOUT RECORD

Checklist Point System:

1–6 points may be awarded by a parent, teacher, or writing coach for each task completed. Here are the recommended guidelines:

6 – exemplary in quality *and* effort

5 – exemplary in either quality *or* effort

4 – acceptable in quality *and* effort

3 – acceptable in either quality *or* effort

2 – needs improvement in quality *and* effort

1 – incomplete

Checklist for Module 3

Directions: When you have completed a task, make a ✔ in the "Done" column. Ask a parent, teacher, or writing coach to award you points for each task using the checklist point system. Fill in the points you have earned on the Journeyman Log in the appendix.

Checklist Point System:

1–6 points may be awarded by a parent, teacher, or writing coach for each task completed. Here are the recommended guidelines:

6 – exemplary in quality *and* effort

5 – exemplary in either quality *or* effort

4 – acceptable in quality *and* effort

3 – acceptable in either quality *or* effort

2 – needs improvement in quality *and* effort

1 – incomplete

Tasks	Done ✔	Points Earned
3.5 When and Where to Cite • Write "yes" or "no" in the column to indicate whether the information must be acknowledged or not.		
3.7 Conventions: Titles • Properly capitalize and format the list of titles.		
• Underline words that should be italicized.		
3.8 Create Your Bibliography • Compile the bibliography for your science report using MLA format (8th edition).		
• Alphabetize your entries.		
3.9 Direct Quotations: Who, Why, When, How • Find at least five possible direct quotations—either spoken or written—you might include in your science report. Make sure each quote contains unique and interesting information or is from a noteworthy individual.		
• Use each possible direct quotation in a sentence that is properly punctuated and cited.		
• Add the information to indicate who said the quote and why the person is qualified or noteworthy.		
3.10 Paraphrase • Discuss the black bear's diet with a parent, teacher, or writing coach.		

Continued on next page »

Tasks	Done ✔	Points Earned
• Paraphrase the information from the listed sources in a paragraph. Try to include complete information about the black bear's diet.		
• Discuss with a parent, teacher, or writing coach how your paraphrase is similar to and different from the expert model.		
3.11 Summarize • Write summary statements about your animal for at least three of the questions listed.		
• Share your summaries with a parent, teacher, or writing coach.		
3.12 The Sandbox • Write a story about your science report animal. It can be a realistic story in which the animal behaves as it does in the wild or an animal fantasy in which the animal can talk and has other human characteristics.		
• Share your story with family and friends.		
3.13 Word Sleuth • List the names of some of the counties, parishes, or boroughs in your state and their centers of government. Add the names of cities and towns to fill the chart, if necessary.		
• Capitalize these place names. They are proper nouns.		
3.14 Revisit: Writer's Questions • Discuss your answers to the Writer's Questions from the beginning of the module with a parent, teacher, or writing coach.		
Total		

Module 3: 108 points possible

Checklist Point System:

1–6 points may be awarded by a parent, teacher, or writing coach for each task completed. Here are the recommended guidelines:

6 – exemplary in quality *and* effort

5 – exemplary in either quality *or* effort

4 – acceptable in quality *and* effort

3 – acceptable in either quality *or* effort

2 – needs improvement in quality *and* effort

1 – incomplete

Checklist for Module 4

Directions: When you have completed a task, make a ✔ in the "Done" column. Ask a parent, teacher, or writing coach to award you points for each task using the checklist point system. Fill in the points you have earned on the JOURNEYMAN LOG in the appendix.

Checklist Point System:

1–6 points may be awarded by a parent, teacher, or writing coach for each task completed. Here are the recommended guidelines:

6 – exemplary in quality *and* effort

5 – exemplary in either quality *or* effort

4 – acceptable in quality *and* effort

3 – acceptable in either quality *or* effort

2 – needs improvement in quality *and* effort

1 – incomplete

Tasks	Done ✔	Points Earned
4.3 Interesting, Original, or Important! • On the chart, list the topics that best answer the questions.		
4.4 Interrogatives Ask Questions • Use interrogative adverbs and interrogative pronouns to form a preliminary list of questions to answer in your science report.		
• Write your preliminary questions on the lines provided.		
4.5 "Into the Wild" Q&A First Draft • Using the expert model in 1.3 and what you learned in module 3, create complete and detailed answers for each of your questions.		
• Practice citing direct quotations and other people's ideas in your draft.		
• Practice combining your research with your own words and original ideas to show off what you have learned. Every answer should be several sentences long. If it is not, you may have to write a broader question to answer.		
4.6 The Order Matters • Organize your list of questions and answers by topics that are related.		
• Choose a question to introduce the topic of your science report.		
• Choose a question that works as a strong conclusion.		
• Show a parent, teacher, or writing coach how you plan to organize your Q&A.		
4.7 Illustrate Your Science Report • Choose several illustrations, photos, maps, or original drawings to include in your science report.		

Continued on next page »

Tasks	Done ✔	Points Earned
• Ask a parent, teacher, or writing coach to show you how to insert these into a computer document or place them in a handwritten report.		
• Write captions for your illustrations and cite the source underneath each one.		
• List the illustrations you have added on the lines provided.		
4.8 Readers Needed • Ask several readers to read your science report and answer a few questions. Use the questions provided to guide your discussion.		
• Decide what feedback you want to incorporate into your final report.		
4.9 Student's Rubric for "Into the Wild" • Before you incorporate feedback from your readers and write the final draft of your science report, study the rubric for this assignment.		
4.10 Finally, Final Draft • Type or handwrite your final version of your science report.		
• Add your complete bibliography to the last page of your report. Make sure you have updated it if necessary.		
• Place the final draft of your science report in your Writer's Portfolio.		
4.11 You Be the Judge • Together with a parent, teacher, or writing coach, use 4.9 Student's Rubric to evaluate the final version of your science report.		
4.12 Word Sleuth • Use a thesaurus to find several synonyms for the words listed. Choose words that are new to you and list them on the chart.		
4.13 Revisit: Writer's Questions • Discuss your answers to the Writer's Questions from the beginning of the module with a parent, teacher, or writing coach.		
Total		

Module 4: 138 points possible

Checklist Point System:

1–6 points may be awarded by a parent, teacher, or writing coach for each task completed. Here are the recommended guidelines:

6 – exemplary in quality *and* effort

5 – exemplary in either quality *or* effort

4 – acceptable in quality *and* effort

3 – acceptable in either quality *or* effort

2 – needs improvement in quality *and* effort

1 – incomplete

Checklist for Module 5

Directions: When you have completed a task, make a ✔ in the "Done" column. Ask a parent, teacher, or writing coach to award you points for each task using the checklist point system. Fill in the points you have earned on the Journeyman Log in the appendix.

Checklist Point System:

1–6 points may be awarded by a parent, teacher, or writing coach for each task completed. Here are the recommended guidelines:

6 – exemplary in quality *and* effort

5 – exemplary in either quality *or* effort

4 – acceptable in quality *and* effort

3 – acceptable in either quality *or* effort

2 – needs improvement in quality *and* effort

1 – incomplete

Tasks	Done ✔	Points Earned
5.4 An Offer You Can't Refuse • Ask at least four people to join you on a dream vacation. List those who accepted your invitation.		
5.6 Generate Your Questions • Think about all the decisions involved in choosing a dream vacation. Add categories of your own to the chart provided.		
• Use the categories on your chart to generate questions for your survey. Create at least one question for each category on the chart.		
5.7 Gather Your Data • Create a chart to record the answers you collect to your survey questions. Read 5.8 Analyze Your Results before you complete the "Best Option" row. Ask every person you have invited on your family vacation the questions on your survey. Record their responses on the chart.		
5.8 Analyze Your Results • Follow the four steps listed to analyze your data. Record the best option at the bottom of each column.		
5.9 Preliminary Ideas • List four characteristics of the place you should find for your family's dream vacation.		
5.10 Interview the Experienced • Schedule interviews with at least two people who have firsthand experience planning a vacation. List their names.		

Continued on next page »

Tasks	Done ✔	Points Earned
• Write some of the questions you will ask at each interview on the lines provided.		
• Conduct your interviews.		
• After each interview, write some of the recommendations people made that you want to research further.		
5.11 Search and Verify • Identify potential destinations that will earn every travel companion's approval. With the help of a parent, teacher, or writing coach, write a list of places to research further.		
• Select and circle the questions you need to answer from the list provided. Write additional questions to research.		
• Ask a parent, teacher, or writing coach to help you use the questions you selected or created to locate reliable and verifiable information on the Internet. List the websites you use to gather this information.		
• Use the chart or create your own to record the answers to your questions and track the information you uncover.		
5.12 You Decide • Write the name of your final choice for your family's dream vacation and explain why you think each of your travel companions will agree with your choice.		
5.13 Word Sleuth • Write synonyms for the words listed.		
5.14 Revisit: Writer's Questions • Discuss your answers to the Writer's Questions from the beginning of the module with a parent, teacher, or writing coach.		
Total		

Module 5: 102 points possible

Checklist Point System:

1–6 points may be awarded by a parent, teacher, or writing coach for each task completed. Here are the recommended guidelines:

6 – exemplary in quality *and* effort

5 – exemplary in either quality *or* effort

4 – acceptable in quality *and* effort

3 – acceptable in either quality *or* effort

2 – needs improvement in quality *and* effort

1 – incomplete

Checklist for Module 6

Directions: When you have completed a task, make a ✔ in the "Done" column. Ask a parent, teacher, or writing coach to award you points for each task using the checklist point system. Fill in the points you have earned on the JOURNEYMAN LOG in the appendix.

Checklist Point System:

1–6 points may be awarded by a parent, teacher, or writing coach for each task completed. Here are the recommended guidelines:

6 – exemplary in quality *and* effort

5 – exemplary in either quality *or* effort

4 – acceptable in quality *and* effort

3 – acceptable in either quality *or* effort

2 – needs improvement in quality *and* effort

1 – incomplete

Tasks	Done ✔	Points Earned
6.3 Six Traits of Good Writing • Study the infographic.		
6.4 An Essay Burger • Study the five body paragraphs on the copy you made of 5.3 EXPERT MODEL and answer the question.		
6.5 Body Paragraphs: Ideas • Locate and underline each topic sentence in your copy of the expert model from 5.3.		
• Fill in the ideas you will include in your body paragraphs in the ARGUMENT ESSAY PARAGRAPH PLANNING CHART. Complete additional research if you realize you need more facts, examples, and details to support your idea.		
6.6 Thesis: The Big Idea • Write a preliminary draft of the thesis you will use to defend your choice for a vacation destination.		
6.7 Body Paragraphs: Organization Again • Discuss the organization of the expert model from 5.3 with a parent, teacher, or writing coach.		
6.9 Blueprint for Success • List the background information, thesis, logical reasons, facts, apt examples, and details you plan to include in the introduction, body paragraphs, and conclusion of your argument essay on the Working Outline work space.		

Continued on next page »

Tasks	Done ✔	Points Earned
6.10 First Draft • Draft your argument essay on paper or the computer. Make several copies to share with some of your readers.		
6.11 Readers Needed • Ask at least three readers to give you feedback on your first draft. Use the suggested questions to guide your discussion.		
• Record some of the most helpful feedback you receive from your readers.		
6.12 Second Draft: Ideas and Organization • Create a second draft of your argument essay using the feedback you received from your readers and your own insights.		
6.13 Word Sleuth • Fill out the chart provided with vocabulary words that are new to you or rarely used words that describe or are examples of the category listed. Try to use the words in discussions about your destination with your family.		
6.14 Revisit: Writer's Questions • Discuss your answers to the Writer's Questions from the beginning of the module with a parent, teacher, or writing coach.		
Total		

Module 6: 78 points possible

Checklist Point System:

1–6 points may be awarded by a parent, teacher, or writing coach for each task completed. Here are the recommended guidelines:

6 – exemplary in quality *and* effort

5 – exemplary in either quality *or* effort

4 – acceptable in quality *and* effort

3 – acceptable in either quality *or* effort

2 – needs improvement in quality *and* effort

1 – incomplete

Checklist for Module 7

Directions: When you have completed a task, make a ✔ in the "Done" column. Ask a parent, teacher, or writing coach to award you points for each task using the checklist point system. Fill in the points you have earned on the Journeyman Log in the appendix.

Checklist Point System:

1–6 points may be awarded by a parent, teacher, or writing coach for each task completed. Here are the recommended guidelines:

6 – exemplary in quality *and* effort

5 – exemplary in either quality *or* effort

4 – acceptable in quality *and* effort

3 – acceptable in either quality *or* effort

2 – needs improvement in quality *and* effort

1 – incomplete

Tasks	Done ✔	Points Earned
7.3 Quick Review • Review and discuss the job of each grammatical unit with a parent, teacher, or writing coach.		
7.5 Sentence Building • Write six sturdy sentences about two lively characters using the sentence parts provided.		
7.6 Review: Subject Complements • Add subjects and the type of complements indicated below the lines to complete the sentences.		
7.7 Verb Complements: Direct Objects • Complete the sentences with verb complements. Mark the direct objects in each verb complement with "D.O."		
7.8 Verb Complements: Indirect Objects • Label direct objects with "D.O." and indirect objects with "I.O." in the sentences. Underline the complete verb complement in each sentence.		
7.9 You Can Do This! • Complete the sentences with the missing sentence parts.		
• Choose and write the correct job of the sentence part above each underlined word or phrase in the sentences.		

Continued on next page »

Tasks	Done ✔	Points Earned
7.10 Mastery Test • Create sentences that follow the specified sentence patterns.		
7.11 Word Sleuth • Complete the columns with verbs beginning with the letter at the top of each column. Choose verbs you do not often use in your writing but would like to use in the future. Use a dictionary or a thesaurus to help you find new verbs to try in your writing. Share your list with a parent, teacher, or writing coach.		
7.12 Revisit: Writer's Questions • Discuss your answers to the Writer's Questions from the beginning of the module with a parent, teacher, or writing coach.		
Total		

Module 7: 60 points possible

Checklist Point System:

1–6 points may be awarded by a parent, teacher, or writing coach for each task completed. Here are the recommended guidelines:

6 – exemplary in quality *and* effort

5 – exemplary in either quality *or* effort

4 – acceptable in quality *and* effort

3 – acceptable in either quality *or* effort

2 – needs improvement in quality *and* effort

1 – incomplete

Checklist for Module 8

Directions: When you have completed a task, make a ✔ in the "Done" column. Ask a parent, teacher, or writing coach to award you points for each task using the checklist point system. Fill in the points you have earned on the JOURNEYMAN LOG in the appendix.

Checklist Point System:

1–6 points may be awarded by a parent, teacher, or writing coach for each task completed. Here are the recommended guidelines:

6 – exemplary in quality *and* effort

5 – exemplary in either quality *or* effort

4 – acceptable in quality *and* effort

3 – acceptable in either quality *or* effort

2 – needs improvement in quality *and* effort

1 – incomplete

Tasks	Done ✔	Points Earned
8.3 A Writer's Fingerprints • Describe the kind of personality you think the writer of the expert model has. List clues from his essay.		
8.4 Voice: Give Me Some Attitude • Rewrite the introduction to your argument essay with two different types of tone.		
8.5 Voice: Show Your Emotions • Revise a paragraph of your argument essay other than the introduction using punctuation, short sentences, and positive descriptive words to convey your emotions.		
8.7 Third Draft: Revise for Voice • Focus on creating a consistent voice as you write the third draft of your argument essay. Ask someone who hasn't already read your argument to read it and answer the question.		
8.8 Inspect and Improve: Sentence Structure • Answer the questions about the sentences from the expert model.		
• List some of the words and phrases you find in your sentences that fit each job description on the chart provided. Discuss your choices with a parent, teacher, or writing coach.		
• Check each sentence from your essay for clarity by answering each question in your mind. Then revise each sentence until the answer for each question is yes.		

Continued on next page »

Tasks	Done ✔	Points Earned
8.9 Inspect and Improve: Nouns • Complete the chart with some of the nouns you find in the expert model in 5.3.		
• Write some of the nouns you currently have in your essay in the first column. Then choose more specific nouns and write those in the second column. Then revise your essay using some of the nouns you listed in the second column.		
8.10 Inspect and Improve: Verbs • Inspect and improve the verbs in your argument essay by adding and revising your action words.		
8.11 Inspect and Improve: Modifiers • Inspect and improve the adjectives and adverbs in your argument essay.		
8.12 Inspect and Improve: Conventions • With the help of a parent, teacher, or writing coach, review and revise as necessary the capitalization, punctuation, spelling, and usage in your argument essay. Ask the adult who is helping you to explain the reason for the change. Or look up the rules that apply in a grammar reference book or a reliable online source together.		
8.13 Student's Rubric for "Making the Case" • Study the rubric for your argument essay before writing your fourth draft.		
8.14 With Fanfare and Panache • Write the fourth draft of your argument essay.		
• Present your argument essay to your traveling companions. Revise your essay as needed until everyone agrees with your recommendation for a dream vacation.		

Continued on next page »

Checklist Point System:

1–6 points may be awarded by a parent, teacher, or writing coach for each task completed. Here are the recommended guidelines:

6 – exemplary in quality *and* effort

5 – exemplary in either quality *or* effort

4 – acceptable in quality *and* effort

3 – acceptable in either quality *or* effort

2 – needs improvement in quality *and* effort

1 – incomplete

Checklist Point System:

1–6 points may be awarded by a parent, teacher, or writing coach for each task completed. Here are the recommended guidelines:

6 – exemplary in quality *and* effort

5 – exemplary in either quality *or* effort

4 – acceptable in quality *and* effort

3 – acceptable in either quality *or* effort

2 – needs improvement in quality *and* effort

1 – incomplete

Tasks	Done ✔	Points Earned
8.15 Finally, Final Draft • If necessary, type or handwrite your final version of your argument essay. Place your paper in your Writer's Portfolio.		
8.16 You Be the Judge • Together with a parent, teacher, or writing coach, use 8.13 Student's Rubric to evaluate the final version of your argument essay.		
8.17 Word Sleuth • Go over your recent research and assignments and list some of the new words you want to continue using in your writing on the lines provided.		
8.18 Revisit: Writer's Questions • Discuss your answers to the Writer's Questions from the beginning of the module with a parent, teacher, or writing coach.		
Total		

Module 8: 114 points possible

Checklist for Module 9

Directions: When you have completed a task, make a ✔ in the "Done" column. Ask a parent, teacher, or writing coach to award you points for each task using the checklist point system. Fill in the points you have earned on the Journeyman Log in the appendix.

Tasks	Done ✔	Points Earned
9.3 What Makes a Poem a Poem? • Read aloud and discuss the poems with a parent, teacher, or writing coach.		
• Describe some of the things you noticed about poetry from studying the poems.		
9.6 Acrostic Poems • Read the two examples of acrostic poems aloud. Listen to how each line sounds and think about the ideas each poem expresses.		
• Read "A Boat Beneath a Sunny Sky" aloud and reflect on the questions.		
• Choose a word or phrase from one of the listed categories and create an acrostic poem about it, making the word or phrase easily visible.		
9.7 The Sound of Music • Sing the long and short vowel sounds and try to sing the sounds of the listed consonants. Say the listed words fast and then slowly, noticing that you must sustain the vowel sounds in order to say them slowly.		
• Think of words that rhyme with the listed words and write them in the chart.		
• Write an alliterative sentence for each of the listed words.		
• List words that repeat the final consonant sound of each word on the chart without repeating the vowel sound.		
• Write sentences that repeat the listed vowel sounds.		
• Memorize "The Eagle" and recite it for your family and friends.		

Checklist Point System:

1–6 points may be awarded by a parent, teacher, or writing coach for each task completed. Here are the recommended guidelines:

6 – exemplary in quality *and* effort

5 – exemplary in either quality *or* effort

4 – acceptable in quality *and* effort

3 – acceptable in either quality *or* effort

2 – needs improvement in quality *and* effort

1 – incomplete

Continued on next page »

Checklist Point System:

1–6 points may be awarded by a parent, teacher, or writing coach for each task completed. Here are the recommended guidelines:

6 – exemplary in quality *and* effort

5 – exemplary in either quality *or* effort

4 – acceptable in quality *and* effort

3 – acceptable in either quality *or* effort

2 – needs improvement in quality *and* effort

1 – incomplete

Tasks	Done ✔	Points Earned
9.8 Expert Model • Recite the stanzas from "Jabberwocky" in your best dramatic voice.		
• Answer the questions about the sound devices in "A Boat Beneath a Sunny Sky."		
9.10 A Melodious, Euphonious Poem • Think about some of your favorite memories from any time in your life. Ask yourself questions to see how many details you can recall about each memory. Select three memories and complete the chart with all the details.		
9.11 A Mysterious Art • Write the memory you will use for your lyric poem. Briefly explain why you chose this memory.		
9.12 Poets Show But Don't Tell Too • Work on the first draft of your poem in parts, remembering to show but not tell readers how you feel about this memory.		
9.13 Revise for Sound • Add sound devices to your poem, reading the drafts aloud until you like the way the poem sounds.		
9.14 Word Sleuth • Find words to use in your writing that answer the questions.		
9.15 Revisit: Writer's Questions • Discuss your answers to the WRITER'S QUESTIONS from the beginning of the module with a parent, teacher, or writing coach.		
Total		

Module 9: 114 points possible

Checklist for Module 10

Directions: When you have completed a task, make a ✔ in the "Done" column. Ask a parent, teacher, or writing coach to award you points for each task using the checklist point system. Fill in the points you have earned on the JOURNEYMAN LOG in the appendix.

Tasks	Done ✔	Points Earned
10.3 The Rhythm of Poetry • Put your hand under your chin and say the words. Underline the stressed part of each word.		
• Try to identify the stressed syllable in each word by saying the words aloud. Underline the stressed syllable of each word and then check your guess with a dictionary.		
10.5 Repetition—A Poet's Friend • Fill out the chart with some of the repeated words and phrases you notice in the poems.		
10.6 Revise for Sound and Rhythm • Revise your acrostic and lyric poems, focusing on improving the sound and meter in both.		
10.7 Haiku U. • Compose a haiku based on a single image or experience. Choose words with vowels to create sound devices. Use nouns and verbs to create stressed and unstressed words.		
10.8 Cinquain Train • Answer the questions about the cinquains by Adelaide Crapsey.		
• Write a cinquain that describes an object, image, or momentary experience that you find striking.		
10.9 Word Sleuth • Find and list at least five new vocabulary words that contain the vowel sound listed at the top of each column in the chart.		
10.10 Revisit: Writer's Questions • Discuss your answers to the WRITER'S QUESTIONS from the beginning of the module with a parent, teacher, or writing coach.		
Total		

Module 10: 54 points possible

Checklist Point System:

1–6 points may be awarded by a parent, teacher, or writing coach for each task completed. Here are the recommended guidelines:

6 – exemplary in quality *and* effort

5 – exemplary in either quality *or* effort

4 – acceptable in quality *and* effort

3 – acceptable in either quality *or* effort

2 – needs improvement in quality *and* effort

1 – incomplete

Checklist for Module 11

Directions: When you have completed a task, make a ✔ in the "Done" column. Ask a parent, teacher, or writing coach to award you points for each task using the checklist point system. Fill in the points you have earned on the Journeyman Log in the appendix.

Checklist Point System:

1–6 points may be awarded by a parent, teacher, or writing coach for each task completed. Here are the recommended guidelines:

6 – exemplary in quality *and* effort

5 – exemplary in either quality *or* effort

4 – acceptable in quality *and* effort

3 – acceptable in either quality *or* effort

2 – needs improvement in quality *and* effort

1 – incomplete

Tasks	Done ✔	Points Earned
11.2 Review Your Progress • Study the list of job descriptions for sentence parts.		
• Fill in the blanks to make the sentences complete and accurate.		
• Answer the questions about the lines of poetry.		
11.3 Language of the Trade • Review the grammatical units you have learned about so far. Circle the ones you know the most about and underline the ones you want to understand better.		
11.4 Pronouns: Function Words • Study the Pronouns chart and try to use each pronoun in a sentence. State each sentence you compose aloud to yourself. Think about the kinds of sentences that use each pronoun.		
11.5 Antecedents • Underline the pronoun that is used with an antecedent in each sentence. Draw an arrow from the pronoun to its antecedent.		
11.6 Personal Pronouns • Complete the sentences by filling each blank with a personal pronoun that makes each sentence grammatically correct.		
• Write sentences of your own using all of the personal pronouns on the chart at least once, remembering to use an antecedent in your sentences when required.		

Continued on next page »

Tasks	Done ✔	Points Earned
11.7 Possessive Pronoun or Possessive Adjective? • Decide if each italicized word in each example is a pronoun or an adjective. Write "Pro." above the pronouns and "Adj." above the adjectives.		
11.8 Pronouns in Poetry • Review the poems you are writing for this unit. Underline the personal and possessive pronouns you use in each poem, and be sure the antecedent for each pronoun is clearly stated in the title or somewhere else in each poem.		
11.9 Point of View • Review the poems you are writing in this unit, examining the pronouns you use. Ask a parent, teacher, or writing coach to help you make sure you have a consistent point of view.		
11.10 The Sandbox • Write a humorous poem, experimenting with sound, meter, and point of view. Read it aloud to your family and friends, noticing the lines that make them smile or laugh.		
11.11 Word Sleuth • Use a dictionary and a box of crayons to fill in the chart with new color words and their definitions.		
11.12 Revisit: Writer's Questions • Discuss your answers to the Writer's Questions from the beginning of the module with a parent, teacher, or writing coach.		
Total		

Module 11: 84 points possible

Checklist Point System:

1–6 points may be awarded by a parent, teacher, or writing coach for each task completed. Here are the recommended guidelines:

6 – exemplary in quality *and* effort

5 – exemplary in either quality *or* effort

4 – acceptable in quality *and* effort

3 – acceptable in either quality *or* effort

2 – needs improvement in quality *and* effort

1 – incomplete

Checklist for Module 12

Directions: When you have completed a task, make a ✔ in the "Done" column. Ask a parent, teacher, or writing coach to award you points for each task using the checklist point system. Fill in the points you have earned on the Journeyman Log in the appendix.

Checklist Point System:

1–6 points may be awarded by a parent, teacher, or writing coach for each task completed. Here are the recommended guidelines:

6 – exemplary in quality *and* effort

5 – exemplary in either quality *or* effort

4 – acceptable in quality *and* effort

3 – acceptable in either quality *or* effort

2 – needs improvement in quality *and* effort

1 – incomplete

Tasks	Done ✔	Points Earned
12.3 The Inventiveness of Poetry • Determine the answers to the questions that correspond to each line of "A Boat Beneath a Sunny Sky."		
12.4 Denotations and Connotations of Words • Fill in the chart with synonyms with both positive and negative connotations that are similar in denotative meaning to each word listed.		
• Study your lyric poem and answer the questions about the connotations of the words you have selected. Ask a parent, teacher, or writing coach to help you use your answers to revise your poem by adding more words rich in connotations.		
12.5 Metaphor and Simile • Answer the questions about the two poems you read.		
• Find and write two similes and one metaphor from the poem. Then describe the two things being compared in each example and choose a title for the poem.		
12.6 Allusion Infusion • Answer the questions about allusions in the sentences.		

Continued on next page »

Tasks	Done ✔	Points Earned
• Read the entire poem "A Boat Beneath a Sunny Sky" aloud again. Answer the questions.		
12.7 The Sandbox • Create similes and metaphors that describe some of your family members, friends, and pets.		
12.9 How to Read a Poem • Use the punctuation guidelines to read the poems aloud. Then place a check mark beside each one you successfully read according to the punctuation signals.		
12.10 Student's Rubrics for "Poetry Jam" • Before writing the final drafts of your four poems, study the rubrics.		
12.11 Finally, Final Drafts • In each poem, make sure you use words with connotative values that contribute to the emotions you want to express.		
• In your lyric poem or cinquain, look for a place to include at least one allusion.		
• In all poems, look for places to add metaphors or similes to better express your ideas.		
• In all poems, add punctuation and capitalization to show where your complete thoughts begin and end, and to show readers how your poem should be read aloud. Put the final draft of each poem in your Writer's Portfolio.		
12.12 Poetry Jam • Practice reading your poems aloud until you have the sound and rhythm perfected.		

Continued on next page »

Checklist Point System:

1–6 points may be awarded by a parent, teacher, or writing coach for each task completed. Here are the recommended guidelines:

6 – exemplary in quality *and* effort

5 – exemplary in either quality *or* effort

4 – acceptable in quality *and* effort

3 – acceptable in either quality *or* effort

2 – needs improvement in quality *and* effort

1 – incomplete

Checklist Point System:

1–6 points may be awarded by a parent, teacher, or writing coach for each task completed. Here are the recommended guidelines:

6 – exemplary in quality *and* effort

5 – exemplary in either quality *or* effort

4 – acceptable in quality *and* effort

3 – acceptable in either quality *or* effort

2 – needs improvement in quality *and* effort

1 – incomplete

Tasks	Done ✔	Points Earned
• Schedule and invite family and friends to a formal reading of your poems. Video record the event to share with others.		
12.13 You Be the Judge • Together with a parent, teacher, or writing coach, use 12.10 Student's Rubrics to evaluate the strengths and weaknesses of your poems.		
12.14 Word Sleuth • Review the poems studied in this unit and list some of the new words found in them on the chart. Add dictionary definitions for each new word.		
• On the second chart, list the best words for each category from the poems in this unit.		
12.15 Revisit: Writer's Questions • Discuss your answers to the Writer's Questions from the beginning of the module with a parent, teacher, or writing coach.		
Total		

Module 12: 120 points possible

Checklist for Module 13

Directions: When you have completed a task, make a ✔ in the "Done" column. Ask a parent, teacher, or writing coach to award you points for each task using the checklist point system. Fill in the points you have earned on the Journeyman Log in the appendix.

Tasks	Done ✔	Points Earned
13.2 Why Imagine? • Talk with a parent, teacher, or writing coach about why you think God gave you an imagination. Take time to thank Him for your fantastic imagination and ask Him to help you use it in new and surprising ways in this unit.		
13.3 The Writing Process • Use the infographic "Introduction to the Writing Process" to answer the questions.		
13.4 Know Your Readers • Name the young listener for whom your story will be written. Include his or her age.		
• Describe some of the things you know about this person. Include some of the books, movies, and activities you know this person likes. If you have a picture of your young listener, then affix it in the space provided.		
13.5 Far and Away • Study the opening pages of a book with a fantastical setting and answer the questions.		
13.6 The Setting Is in the Details • Fill out the Setting chart with some of the ideas you have about your fantastical time and place.		
• After you have decided on some of the details, choose a memorable name for this fantasyland and include it on the Setting chart. Also write the name of the child for whom you are creating this tale.		

Checklist Point System:

1–6 points may be awarded by a parent, teacher, or writing coach for each task completed. Here are the recommended guidelines:

6 – exemplary in quality *and* effort

5 – exemplary in either quality *or* effort

4 – acceptable in quality *and* effort

3 – acceptable in either quality *or* effort

2 – needs improvement in quality *and* effort

1 – incomplete

Continued on next page »

Checklist Point System:

1–6 points may be awarded by a parent, teacher, or writing coach for each task completed. Here are the recommended guidelines:

6 – exemplary in quality *and* effort

5 – exemplary in either quality *or* effort

4 – acceptable in quality *and* effort

3 – acceptable in either quality *or* effort

2 – needs improvement in quality *and* effort

1 – incomplete

Tasks	Done ✔	Points Earned
13.7 A Map to Guide You • Write some of the place names you find and the titles of the books they come from on the Place Names from a Fantastical Setting chart.		
• Make several drafts of a map of the fantastical setting for your fantasy tale. When you have finalized it, draw it in the space provided. Label the bodies of water, mountain ranges, forests, towns, etc. with place names you invent.		
• Share your map with your young listener.		
13.8 Fantastical Creatures Who Walk and Talk • On the Famous Fantastical Villains chart, list some of the famous antagonists you can recall from fantasy or fairy tales. Put a star beside the one you think is the best villain an author has created.		
• List details about each of your major characters on the Character Planning chart.		
13.9 Concoct a Plot • Describe the main problem that must be resolved in your fantastical tale.		
• Use the Plot Stages for My Fantastical Tale chart to show the events that will occur in each stage of your fantastical tale of extraordinary exploits.		
13.10 Word Sleuth • Start a list of words that fit the given criteria. As you work on your story during the rest of the unit, continue to add to this list.		
13.11 Revisit: Writer's Questions • Discuss your answers to the Writer's Questions from the beginning of the module with a parent, teacher, or writing coach.		
Total		

Module 13: 96 points possible

Checklist for Module 14

Directions: When you have completed a task, make a ✔ in the "Done" column. Ask a parent, teacher, or writing coach to award you points for each task using the checklist point system. Fill in the points you have earned on the Journeyman Log in the appendix.

Tasks	Done ✔	Points Earned
14.4 First-Person Point of View • Find a favorite book with a first-person point of view. Page through multiple sections of the book at different stages of the plot, and then answer the questions.		
14.5 Third-Person Point of View • Circle all the personal pronouns and possessive adjectives in the expert model. Label each one first, second, or third person.		
• Rewrite the opening of *Charlotte's Web* from a first-person point of view. Use Fern as the narrator. Include some of what Fern is thinking and feeling.		
• Discuss the possible points of view you might use for your fantastical tale with a parent, teacher, or writing coach. Consider the advantages and limitations of each. When you have decided who will tell your story, explain your choice and the point of view you will use on the lines provided.		
14.6 Give Your Narrator an Attitude • Decide what kind of personality your narrator will have. Decide what character traits you will emphasize and what tone of voice you want your narrator to use as he or she tells the story. Fill out the My Narrator's Voice chart with this information.		

Checklist Point System:

1–6 points may be awarded by a parent, teacher, or writing coach for each task completed. Here are the recommended guidelines:

6 – exemplary in quality *and* effort

5 – exemplary in either quality *or* effort

4 – acceptable in quality *and* effort

3 – acceptable in either quality *or* effort

2 – needs improvement in quality *and* effort

1 – incomplete

Continued on next page »

Checklist Point System:

1–6 points may be awarded by a parent, teacher, or writing coach for each task completed. Here are the recommended guidelines:

6 – exemplary in quality *and* effort

5 – exemplary in either quality *or* effort

4 – acceptable in quality *and* effort

3 – acceptable in either quality *or* effort

2 – needs improvement in quality *and* effort

1 – incomplete

Tasks	Done ✔	Points Earned
14.7 Compare Two Opening Chapters • Choose two books with fantastical settings and read the opening chapter(s) of each or study the first few pages of two picture books. Read each book until you have information for each cell in the Two Opening Chapters chart.		
• Fill out the chart with some of the information you discover in each chapter.		
14.8 First Draft • Work on the first draft of your fantastical tale for at least three days. Write the date and time you worked on your story on the chart. Also note what part of the draft you worked on.		
14.9 Word Sleuth • Create some neologisms. List your new words, their parts of speech, and their definitions on the lines provided. Give an example of how you might use each word in a sentence. Add to this list as you continue to draft your story.		
14.10 Revisit: Writer's Questions • Discuss your answers to the Writer's Questions from the beginning of the module with a parent, teacher, or writing coach.		
Total		

Module 14: 60 points possible

Checklist for Module 15

Directions: When you have completed a task, make a ✔ in the "Done" column. Ask a parent, teacher, or writing coach to award you points for each task using the checklist point system. Fill in the points you have earned on the JOURNEYMAN LOG in the appendix.

Tasks	Done ✔	Points Earned
15.1 Review Your Progress • Study the list of job descriptions and review what you learned about complements in module 7.		
• Fill in the blanks to make the sentences complete and accurate.		
• Answer the questions about personal pronouns and possessive adjectives.		
15.3 Why Pronouns Matter • Cross out the nouns that you think the author replaced with pronouns in the original paragraph.		
• Write the pronoun or possessive adjective you believe the author used above the noun.		
15.4 Reflexive Pronouns • Create six sentences that include reflexive pronouns. Choose a pronoun from each cell on the REFLEXIVE PRONOUNS CHART.		
• Read your sentences to a parent, teacher, or writing coach.		
• Use the chart in 15.1 to help you insert the type of pronoun named below the line in each of the sentences.		
15.5 Indefinite Pronouns • Complete each sentence with an indefinite pronoun. Make sure it agrees with the verb.		
• Complete each sentence with a verb form that agrees with the indefinite pronoun.		
15.6 Demonstrative Pronouns • Write sentences using *this*, *these*, *that*, and *those* as demonstrative pronouns and as demonstrative adjectives.		

Checklist Point System:

1–6 points may be awarded by a parent, teacher, or writing coach for each task completed. Here are the recommended guidelines:

6 – exemplary in quality *and* effort

5 – exemplary in either quality *or* effort

4 – acceptable in quality *and* effort

3 – acceptable in either quality *or* effort

2 – needs improvement in quality *and* effort

1 – incomplete

Continued on next page »

Checklist Point System:

1–6 points may be awarded by a parent, teacher, or writing coach for each task completed. Here are the recommended guidelines:

6 – exemplary in quality *and* effort

5 – exemplary in either quality *or* effort

4 – acceptable in quality *and* effort

3 – acceptable in either quality *or* effort

2 – needs improvement in quality *and* effort

1 – incomplete

Tasks	Done ✔	Points Earned
15.7 Can't We All Agree? • In the sentences, fill in the blank with a pronoun (or adjective formed from a pronoun) that agrees with the antecedent.		
• On the line below each sentence, list three pronouns you can use that agree with the verb.		
• Change the words necessary to make all parts of the sentences agree.		
15.8 The Sandbox • Rewrite a favorite fairy tale or adventure story from another character's perspective. Try to create a distinct tone of voice for the character who tells the story.		
• Share your story with family or friends. Ask them to describe the narrator's tone of voice.		
15.9 Inspect and Improve: Pronouns • Review two completed writing assignments for this volume, plus the first draft of your fantastical tale. Inspect each and every pronoun you can find. Use the checklist to help you identify and fix problems. Ask a parent, teacher, or writing coach to help you.		
15.10 Word Sleuth • With help from a dictionary and the Internet, complete the chart of collective nouns and the groups they describe.		
15.11 Revisit: Writer's Questions • Revisit the WRITER'S QUESTIONS from the beginning of this module. Talk about your answers with a parent, teacher, or writing coach.		
Total		

Module 15: 114 points possible

Checklist for Module 16

Directions: When you have completed a task, make a ✔ in the "Done" column. Ask a parent, teacher, or writing coach to award you points for each task using the checklist point system. Fill in the points you have earned on the Journeyman Log in the appendix.

Tasks	Done ✔	Points Earned
16.3 Be Your Own Reader • Ask yourself the questions about your draft. Review and revise as needed.		
16.4 Recruit Some Expert Readers • Ask several expert readers to read the draft of your fantastical tale. Then have a conversation about what parts each reader likes best and what parts each reader thinks could be improved. Use the questions in 16.3 Be Your Own Reader to guide your discussion.		
• Use the space provided to take notes about their suggestions.		
16.5 Second Draft • Take the best advice you have gathered from your expert readers and write a second draft of your fantastical tale.		
• List some of the ways you used feedback from your own careful review and your expert readers to improve your story.		
16.6 Close Reading: *The Hobbit*, Chapter 1 • Read the opening chapter of *The Hobbit*. Use the Close Reading chart to jot down some of the things you notice in each category.		
16.7 The Hook • Guess the children's story each sentence introduces and think about why these opening lines are memorable. Record your answers in the Famous Opening Lines chart.		
• Examine the opening lines of your fantastical tale. Think about how you grab your readers' attention and describe it.		

Checklist Point System:

1–6 points may be awarded by a parent, teacher, or writing coach for each task completed. Here are the recommended guidelines:

6 – exemplary in quality *and* effort

5 – exemplary in either quality *or* effort

4 – acceptable in quality *and* effort

3 – acceptable in either quality *or* effort

2 – needs improvement in quality *and* effort

1 – incomplete

Continued on next page »

Checklist Point System:

1–6 points may be awarded by a parent, teacher, or writing coach for each task completed. Here are the recommended guidelines:

6 – exemplary in quality *and* effort

5 – exemplary in either quality *or* effort

4 – acceptable in quality *and* effort

3 – acceptable in either quality *or* effort

2 – needs improvement in quality *and* effort

1 – incomplete

Tasks	Done ✔	Points Earned
• If you can tweak your opening to better intrigue your readers, revise it now.		
16.8 Show but Don't Tell • Look at the conversations between characters in your fantastical tale. Rework at least one conversation in your story to show readers more precisely what each character is like and how they differ from one another.		
• Add more details about where and when your fantastical tale takes place. Use dialogue and action to help you give readers more clues about the setting.		
• When you are finished, share your revision with a parent, teacher, or writing coach.		
• Give your characters some distinguishing characteristics and describe some of these in great detail.		
16.9 Vivify Your Voices • Look at the first few pages of *The Hobbit* and the Expert Model as you consider the narrator's voice.		
• Experiment with some of the strategies you learned about in this section by revising your story.		
16.10 Student's Rubric for "A Fantastical Tale of Extraordinary Exploits" • Before you write the final draft of your fantastical tale, study the rubric for this assignment.		
16.11 Finally, Final Draft • Write your final draft of your fantastical tale. Check your grammar, punctuation, spelling, and capitalization. If you are not sure if something is correct, ask a parent, teacher, or writing coach to proofread your story for you. Then study the corrections they make. Find out what rules they are applying.		

Continued on next page »

Tasks	Done ✔	Points Earned
• Review each bulleted point of the rubric carefully as you polish your fantastical tale. Then type your final version of your story on a computer or handwrite it on notebook paper and put it in your Writer's Portfolio.		
• Choose a perfect time to read your story aloud to your younger sibling or friend. Practice reading it aloud a few times. Think about how you can make this a special occasion.		
• Read the story aloud to your listener. When you are finished, ask your listener what he or she enjoyed most about the story.		
16.12 You Be the Judge • Together with a parent, teacher, or writing coach, use 16.10 Student's Rubric to evaluate the strengths and weaknesses of your make-believe tale.		
16.13 Word Sleuth • Go over your work from this unit and add any words you want to remember how to spell correctly to the chart. Also add any new words you have learned in this module or come across in your reading that you want to remember to use in your writing.		
16.14 Revisit: Writer's Questions • Revisit the Writer's Questions from the beginning of this module. Talk about your answers with a parent, teacher, or writing coach.		
Total		

Module 16: 138 points possible

Checklist Point System:

1–6 points may be awarded by a parent, teacher, or writing coach for each task completed. Here are the recommended guidelines:

6 – exemplary in quality *and* effort

5 – exemplary in either quality *or* effort

4 – acceptable in quality *and* effort

3 – acceptable in either quality *or* effort

2 – needs improvement in quality *and* effort

1 – incomplete